Preachers do the CRAZIEST THINGS!

Edwin & Mable Purviance

Published by
Edwin and Mable Purviance
1216 Ponderosa
Missoula, Montana 59802

Printed in the United States of America
by
Express Printing
Missoula, Montana

CONTENTS

CONTENTS (continued)

Page

Remember God's love is
eternal -- Read Romans 8:38,39

Edwin + Mable

Birth of Our Book

This small volume, *Preachers Do the Craziest Things!* is a potpourri--a collection of happenings we've experienced across the years. Once you begin reading, we believe you'll not want to put the book down.

Some incidents will tickle your funny bone while others will take you to the battlegrounds of life where, incredibly, the hand of God stayed the tide of serious harm with the same authority He held back the waters of the Red Sea for the Israelites.

As we have relived certain events--some having occurred early in our ministry, others with the yoke of time upon us--we have put them into book form with the prayerful hope that they will uplift the dispirited and challenge the wavering, encouraging each to seek a closer walk with God. As He shielded us through good times and times not so good, He will keep His watchful eye upon you.

Across the years, we have put the proclamation of the psalmist to the test and have found his assertions hold true:

If I ascend up into heaven, thou art there.... If I take the wings of the morning, and dwell in the uttermost parts of the sea; Even there shall thy hand lead me, and thy right hand shall hold me.

(Psalm 139)

Happy reading to our friends--old ones and perhaps new ones we'll make through the pages of this book.

Edwin and Mable Purviance
1216 Ponderosa Drive
Missoula, Montana 59802

(Autumn, 1993)

Foreword

As the Purviances recount their experiences of fifty years of ministry, their stories will bring you delight, joy, amusement, amazement, sadness, and tears. Through these accounts we are made to realize how God can use faithful servants willing to exercise their talents to affect others around them. We see how God has first place in the Purviances' lives and we can feel the enthusiasm of their faith.

This book will touch your heart and give you a sense of the greatness of God's love for us.

Chris and Nancy Feucht
Physician -- Nurse

and this is the way it happened . . .

Preachers Do the Craziest Things!

(Edwin)

Preachers are a sneaky lot! I'm one of them, and my darling wife is my accomplice.

We had settled into a recently acquired parsonage in South Florida and were comfortably situated--until cold weather struck. Our home was completely devoid of heat, and Florida cold--when it does strike--chills to the bone.

We had broadly hinted to the church trustees our need for some sort of heat, but somehow the matter had remained on a back burner.

One morning Mable unfolded *The Herald.* The masthead gave the weather forecast: "Freezing temperatures by early evening."

"That does it!" I thundered. "We're taking action!"

"Such as?" Mable prodded.

"Have we any ice cream?" I inquired. Mable never fails to tabulate her stock. "Plenty," she responded. "But why?"

"I'm getting every trustee on the phone, calling an 'important' meeting for this evening at the parsonage."

Mable was with me. "And as they arrive I'll insist on taking their coats. But what about the ice cream?"

"We'll want to show hospitality," I explained,

"so after they've spent all evening in this ice box we'll serve them a generous helping of ice cream."

The meeting went well. In fact, so well that early the next morning--before the breakfast dishes had been cleared from the table--I responded to a knock on the parsonage door. There stood two brawny fellows bearing an unwieldy cardboard box.

It contained a huge reverse cycle air conditioner--great against summer heat, but equally effective against winter cold!

Don't preachers do the craziest things!

"Lady, You'll Be Dead before Mornin'!"

(Mable)

Pick *mushrooms?*

I didn't even know the odd–shaped little creatures grew in the Far North! But it sounded like a barrel of fun and I was all for it. I herded the children in from play, collared my husband, and soon everything was GO!

Vi and Vesper, a winsome, God–fearing couple in our church, drove us to their favorite woodland hideaway a few miles from Fairbanks. Then, they showed us how to go about it. I didn't know a mushroom from a toadstool––but I trusted our friends' judgment completely.

"These are edible––these are not," we were instructed and soon all of us were up to our elbows in pure pleasure.

After we had devoured generous samples hot from the skillet and had stashed away even more in our baskets, we were approached by three timorous youngsters who had cautiously crept up to watch the goings on. They stood simply appalled as each of us in our party proceeded to keep his mouth generously supplied.

The tallest of the gawking onlookers, a bit more audacious than his buddies, singled me out.

"Say, lady, you know something?"

"What?" I asked, as I swallowed a mouthful to make speech reasonably intelligible.

"You eatin' them things? Them's poison!" The child allowed sufficient time for his disclosure to sink in, then came forth with his prediction: "Lady, you'll be *dead* before mornin'!"

I appreciated the youngster's forthrightness, and I gathered he was concerned about my brief future. I was sure he was convinced tomorrow's edition of *The Daily News-Miner* would headline the account of a party of foolhardy citizens having succumbed after devouring toadstools.

But as you may have surmised--and as Mark Twain might have put it--any word of our passing away would have been greatly exaggerated!

In the Middle of "Nowhere"

(Mable)

We looked like clowns at a circus--and just about as grubby--as all eleven of us tumbled out of that beat-up old Land Rover.

Edwin and I were really in the boondocks, and in a foreign country at that. We were in the Central American country of Guatemala visiting our corporation's home for destitute children. When we ran out of road--and that's exactly what happened--we left our vehicle and set out on foot to visit the tiny, isolated huts from which our youngsters had come.

Let me explain that some of the children are blessed with living parents, and Edwin and I knew we just must get personally acquainted with at least some of these poverty-stricken people.

A number of the children we had received into our home came from so far back in the hills that in order to reach their miserable little huts we'd have to ride a mule almost a full day. I simply couldn't envision myself astride a mule all those hours and I "chickened out" on visiting any place that remote. Where we DID end up was far enough from civilization to suit me!

Have you ever ridden--I'm sure you have NOT!--in a Land Rover with ten others? I facetiously referred to our means of travel as a glorified Jeep, although there certainly was no glory derived from riding in THAT thing! And especially over tortuous, dust-caked roads! Several children we care for in our orphanage, along with adult workers, accompanied us. Without the children's guidance we would never have found their parents' home--and, besides, I just loved each of those little ones. They were such dear children that I just wanted to squeeze them.

I even loved the one who--well, shall we say got car sick? Every time we rounded a curve in the road the child threw up. The first occurrence led to a quick inventory and a discovery of one somewhat soiled Kleenex. We cleaned up the poor little thing the best we could, but that was just the beginning. My dear husband fished from his pocket a white handkerchief, and the consensus was that since it was *his* handkerchief he should preside over the mopping up. Believe me, it was a constant job! Added to this was the fact that heavy dust on the road made it impossible for us to roll down a window. I must say the air DID get a bit-- well, to be perfectly honest, it was stinky!

As we departed the Land Rover we began marching single file through an endless expanse of corn fields. I just couldn't fathom how anyone could keep his bearings because every corn stalk looked exactly like the last one--and we trudged past thousands. A more bedraggled procession--hot, dusty, and dead tired--could not have been equaled *anywhere!* I confessed to Edwin who trekked right behind me, "I'm so thirsty I'd settle for ditch water." Of course, I didn't actually mean it.

What we discovered in those tiny, windowless huts made me forget I ever had a problem. The huts were windowless to keep out "evil spirits", therefore light and ventilation came in only through the door which was perhaps 48 inches high. Water in the hills was--and I'm sure still is--precious to the last drop. I discovered it was a three-hour journey each way just to fetch a couple of buckets. When I beheld the primitive living conditions under which these people lived--isolated for days at a time during the rainy season, living at an elevation above eight thousand feet, and of course electricity was unheard of--it made me positively ashamed that I ever complained about anything.

One by one, all eleven of us grabbed our knees and waddled inside the little home from which one of our precious little girls had come. Family ties are strong among the hill people, and the blind father, mother, older sister, and grandmother staged a celebration that touched my heart. They longed to have the young child back home, but--far more-- they coveted for her the chance in life she was receiving. I could have used a Kleenex (remember?), but what really released the tears was the hospitality of the child's father. Would you believe he offered each of us a share of the family's priceless commodity: WATER! Of course we suddenly found we were not thirsty in the least!

As I trudged once again through the trackless fields of grain back to our transportation I was suddenly overtaken by a wave of homesickness. I simply hungered to return to my own prosperous nation and paint word pictures wherever possible of such loving, deserving, but penniless, people.

Today, my mind raced through a mere

fraction of my countless blessings: when I turn on my faucet for a shower--when I flip the electric switch to flood my kitchen with light--when I merely raise a window or open wide a door--when I go to my refrig for "makings" for the next meal-- when I drive on wide, paved highways--I am amid opulence beyond the wildest dreams of my Guatemalan brothers and sisters. It's time for me to seek more means of making life richer for others.

Dear God, show me the way!

The Boy Who "Read" His Bible

(Mable)

He was in his early teens and as faithful to our church as a person could be.

During our week of revival, the congregation was requested to make a special effort to read the Scriptures. Every night during services we tallied up the total number of Bible chapters read by our parishioners during the day. And every night the youngster far outshone all others. He reported *twenty chapters* read. WOW! What devotion! One hundred chapters read during the week! However, on the final night the truth was out. The keen young fellow had turned each day to Psalm 117. And each day he had read it twenty times.

The psalm has but *two verses!*

From the Jaws of Death

(Edwin)

"I just phoned to say 'Good-by.'"

The hour was late but bright as noonday that summer evening in the Far North when Mable picked up the phone. Immediately, she recognized the voice on the other end of the wire. Ted Morris, a hulking sort, in his middle years, apparently was leaving, but where on earth was he headed at this hour?

Mable put that question to Ted. "I'm going away," he responded in his Southern drawl. Ted had migrated from deep-South to Far North. "I'm endin' it all--with this shotgun sittin' right across my knees!"

Her mind racing with prayer for wisdom, Mable beckoned me to her side. "It's Ted Morris," she whispered, covering the mouthpiece. "Has a shotgun across his knees and vows he's about to use it--on himself! Get going, honey!"

In a matter of seconds I was racing across town. "Lord, just don't let Ted hang up that phone....Keep Mable talking....Thank You we were home when Ted called....Don't let me have an accident....And, Lord, grant me wisdom!" It was the most disjointed prayer ever uttered, but I decided long ago God gives ear to any prayer coming from a sincere heart.

The late evening sun was streaming through

Ted's open door as I ground to a halt.   Sure enough, there he sat in a straight chair, gun resting across his knees--but with an ear still glued to the phone! "Thank You, Lord!" I breathed, wondering what my dear wife had found to talk about just to keep Ted on the line. Later, she confessed she did not remember.

As I approached the door, trying to assume a casual pace, I heard Ted drawl: "Somebody's at the door so I'm hangin' up. Now don't try to call me back 'cause I won't be around to answer!"

Ted didn't invite me to sit down--I just did it anyway. Acting as though I supposed he was simply cleaning his gun, I began a casual conversation, as light as though we were at the ball park. Then, I steered our small talk around to Ted's belief in Jesus and His saving power, and I brought up the fact that Ted had meant much to me personally as well as to the church. I recounted a number of occasions when he showed up just when I needed him. Ted seemed pleased. One summer he had managed the church softball team.

When I broached the subject of the gun, Ted made his confession. Yes, he had planned to use it on himself, but now--well, maybe it wasn't such a good idea. We spent a long evening together but every minute seemed well invested as a gradual change settled over this hulking steam fitter. The breakthrough became apparent when Ted extended his hand--as huge as a ham--engulfing mine. It was time for prayer--a victory prayer. In crises such as these, incorporating Scripture into one's prayer contributes much to the effectiveness. Consider one or more of the following verses:

Of course, there's an unlimited reservoir of Scripture verses one may wish to choose from, to call upon in crisis times. Also, it's extremely helpful to bear in mind the fact that when we quote Scripture, Satan leaves us alone--at least, as Luke's Gospel affirms, "for a season" (4:13).

Now in a rational state of mind and with no future intentions of harming himself, Ted Morris stashed away his gun, promising never to consider using it again.

Years have passed and Ted has remained true to his commitment.

God has rewarded His servant Ted with a closer walk with Him, with invaluable service to the church, and--in later years--with a loving, compassionate helpmate to bless his home and his life.

The Man Who Kept His Promise

(Edwin)

He was a man of his word--well, sort of!

During seminary days my very young wife and I traveled well back into the Georgia countryside every Sunday morning to serve a small white church "a stone's throw from Stone Mountain." Our parishioners were kindly folk living in the farming community.

Among the worshipers was a sprinkling of singles. William was among the more faithful ones. A likable young chap of thirty, William lived at home with his father.

In answer to my query about his father attending worship services, William's assurance was always the same: "He'll be here, preacher. He said to tell you he'll be here just as soon as he gets straightened out. Yes sir, just as soon as he gets straightened out he'll be here!" All during the year I received the same response: "... just as soon as he gets straightened out!"

Word reached me one day that the elderly man had died. The funeral director prepared the body for burial, placed it in a casket, and dispatched it to the church for services.

Sure enough, the old fellow proved true to his word: *just as soon as he got straightened out-- he was there!*

It Was Now--or Never

(Mable)

"You want to go *where*--and do *what?*"

Lord, how do I handle this? I bombarded heaven! My husband's parents and my own parents--perched like birds about to take wing-- were on the edge of their seats in our Florida parsonage living room. Though it was winter, the warm day allowed gentle zephyrs to flow in and out of our home.

One of the dads was making a valiant attempt to bridle David, our three-year-old bundle of wiggles, while one of the mothers cuddled Evelyn, our tiny tot who had just triumphantly taken her first step.

I drew in a deep breath. I was about to launch a bombshell--and I must say it was a shocker!

"Mothers and dads," I began, as I looked into four pairs of anxious eyes, "I must tell you. Our family is moving to northern Alaska. Edwin and I feel called to serve God as missionaries in the Far North." That was all I said.

I felt almost criminal, I really did. I think I could have announced I had contracted leprosy and was being sent somewhere to a lonely island and the effect would have been no more devastating.

No one moved. I wondered if everyone was

still breathing. I was sure each one was conjuring up all sorts of images: windblown snow would build up to the rooftops; we'd probably lose our sanity in a one-room igloo (actually, there are no igloos in Alaska); a dog team of snarling huskies would be our sole means of transportation; and a platter of whale blubber would grace our table as our daily fare. Was anyone *ever* going to respond?

After an eternity, Edwin's dad spoke in a strained voice, barely audible. In but half a dozen words he finalized the matter, at least for him: "Well, we'll never see you again!" At the same instant he gave our small son, upon whom he just doted, a heartrending little squeeze.

I knew each was suffering--a great deal. But this was God's call upon us and we could not be deterred. Most of my life I've striven to cut my spiritual garments by the pattern of the Apostle Paul: "...do I seek to please men? for if I yet pleased men, I should not be the servant of Christ" (Galatians 1:10). And for as long as I can remember, I claimed Jesus' final promise before the Ascension: "...and, lo, I am with you alway, even unto the end of the world" (Matthew 28:20).

And so--we went, a bit apprehensively, I must confess, but we went--the four of us.

Problems? The place crawled with them! Just to recall a few: alcoholism, divorce, swapping of marriage partners, homicides, prostitution, and loneliness. Even an escaped prisoner from Georgia was in our congregation. And why did he remain free? Because he had crossed so many states and traveled so far that the long arm of the law was not *that* long. And if our Lord forgave him and offered him another chance, why shouldn't we?

Despite Satan's strangle hold on the Far North, our missionary years were among our most productive. Have you noticed how God always provides a nucleus of faithful people wherever He plants a church? We found this so everywhere we turned.

Our family was never healthier. Evelyn--suffering from bronchitis in Florida--never had an attack in that cold climate. And David was down only long enough to lose his tonsils.

Long ago, I decided that if we follow God's leading--with no reservations--He'll walk before us, beside us, and behind us. And do you know, I am convinced all of us are missionaries! You may not trudge several thousand miles to some bleak outpost in order to meet His call. More likely, it will be across the street or around the block. God knows exactly where He wants you. But do *you* know?

I just can't read our Lord's Words without blushing with contrition that I have not done more. He said, "The harvest truly is plenteous, but the labourers are few" (Matthew 9:37). And even that forlorn ancient prophet, Jeremiah, pricks my conscience at times. Hear his words: "The harvest is past, the summer is ended, and we are not saved" (8:20).

And now--if you will excuse me--I think I hear my Father calling. I believe He has work for me to do!

Stars will not forever shine,
     Nor mountain peaks endure;
But this, a lesson man need learn:
     Christ's promises are sure!

Shepherds, Wise Men, and Tricycles

(Mable)

Talk about drama! This was it !

All these years, you've probably believed the Wise Men from the East reached Bethlehem astride their camels. Would you believe they journeyed to the manger aboard tricycles? That's really the way it was--if you're willing to stretch your imagination far enough.

Edwin and I care for a small army of darling little cripples through our charitable organization, World's Children, Inc. The tiny tads in our Japanese orphanage are a rueful patchwork of contorted little bodies, encasing young hearts which hunger for a smothering hug and for an assurance that somebody loves them. Of course, once adjusted in our orphanage all doubt is removed.

The Christmas Season has rolled around and the little dears have just heard the Christmas story. Nothing will do but to reenact the Biblical account--with *them* as the all-star cast! What if those tiny frames are contorted, each youngster must be assigned a part in the drama. To overlook even one would bring about a crushed heart.

As the curtain opens, Joseph and Mary have already been placed on the stage, as have the little lambs encircling the créche, each exhibiting an ecstasy that forces a tear or two to course down the cheeks of the audience.

As for the shepherds and the wise men, they have not yet arrived. The shepherds, crook in one hand and crutch in the other, begin the endless trek down the aisle toward the stage--at a snail's pace while an eternity passes--but who's to hurry them? It's their moment and the spotlight is upon them! Pathetic? Perish the thought! It's the proudest moment of their young lives!

At long last the Magi head toward "Bethlehem." Possessed of spindly legs incapable of supporting their frail little bodies, they almost burst with pride as they journey toward the manger, each astride his trusted mount--not a camel of course but a tricycle! It calls for one's imagination but--after all--isn't that what imagination is for? And if it brings into focus a sense of belonging, a feeling of recognition, that's all that is necessary.

Being converted into a Bethlehem shepherd or a much-traveled wise man for a fleeting span of time may seem of small consequence. But the angels themselves must surely have smiled upon each precious little moppet. And I'm rather certain there would have been only mild surprise had there been an actual reenactment of that first heavenly host scene among the shepherds outside Bethlehem, accompanied by a burst of fervor:

Glory to God in the highest, and on earth peace, good will toward men (Luke 2:14).

And I'm equally sure this tired, bruised world could do with a bit more of the innocence of childhood: a potpourri of humility and pride blended with a sense of being needed by hurting humanity.

Jesus and Children

Have you ever noticed how much attention our Lord devoted to children? What a contrast to our way! With tiring regularity we discover we are "too busy" or "too weary"--or simply "too important." But Jesus never was. I cringe every time I read of how the disciples shunted some little ones aside as though to say, "Can't you see that Jesus is too busy to be concerned with children?" But then I take delight in reading how our Lord answered the question, "Who is the greatest in the kingdom of heaven? And Jesus called a little child unto him, and set him in the midst of them, and said, ...Except ye...become as little children, ye shall not enter into the kingdom of heaven" (Matthew 18:1-3). Let's remember there's a vast difference between being *childlike*--and being *childish!*

How our Lord must be hurt these days by the manner in which little children are abused! I simply ache when the news media inform me of the barbaric cruelty meted out to defenseless little ones. Jesus said it is better for such offenders to be "drowned in the depth of the sea" (Matthew 18:6). Harsh treatment? Our Lord didn't think so! He said a millstone should be tied about the offender's neck! For clarity, we might say "a very heavy stone" used in grinding grain.

By contrast, I want to share with you an example of what I consider Christlike concern, demonstrated by a young mother for her child. When her lively offspring came charging up to her he was simply bursting with pride over the creation he had put on paper. Never had Rembrandt done better! The mother might have brushed him off with a tart, "Show me later, honey--I'm busy!" She did not do this. She might have given the treasured work of art a cursory glance, then quashed the child's enthusiasm as she inquired--as I'm afraid I would have done!--"What on earth is it?" Instead, she devoted full attention to her child, not sure what it was but urging, "Honey, tell me about it!" What a beautiful relationship between mother and child!

I was similarly blessed--although the situation was heartrending--that early spring morning Jan phoned from the Fairbanks funeral home. She called to say that two small boys--neither yet in his teens--had been flown in from Kotzebue, an Eskimo community out on the bleak wind-swept Arctic coast. The poor little tykes had consumed a quantity of antifreeze and the older had succumbed. Jan informed me he was wearing nothing but a pair of ratty old jeans.

"Mable," she confided, "I just couldn't do it. Even in death I just couldn't. No one would have known--but I just couldn't do it. I couldn't seal that little casket that way!" *Bless, you Jan,* I thought.

Several friends and I went into action, scrounging about until we came up with a manly looking outfit for the unfortunate child. Jan then shipped his body back to Kotzebue for burial. It seemed so little, yet we saw it as a God-given opportunity to demonstrate love for one of Jesus' precious little children.

Opportunities for ministering to His little ones are simply endless! I'm certain that, if we ask Him, our Lord will open doors for each of us to touch the lives of those about us--especially His hurting children. What a marvelous way to work with Him in bringing about a better world!

"How Many Make 'Enough'?"

(Edwin)

Words are like feathers in the wind: once released they can never be recalled!

Embarrassment, hurt feelings, schisms, and broken lives have resulted from words ill spoken. As a preacher I plead guilty, and as a preacher I confess preachers do and say the craziest things!

During seminary days I was assigned to four churches, one far back in the boondocks. The little white building boasted neither electricity nor running water, and winter rains quickly turned the road into a quagmire. Services were conducted one Sunday a month, morning and evening.

When my car bogged down a mile from my appointment one Sunday morning I trekked the remaining distance, trousers rolled to my knees and tennis shoes upon my feet. Following the service, half a dozen stalwart parishioners grunted and groaned behind my car until it rested on firmer ground. A genial couple invited me to Sunday dinner, and I was expected to remain in their home until time for evening worship.

Toward evening, the relentless rain still falling, I cast apprehensive glances out the window, then announced to my host and hostess that I had decided to head for home. My kindly host--simply astounded by my decision--gave me an incredulous look, at the same time asking, "What about evening worship?"

I had thought about that--in fact, little else --all that dreary afternoon. I replied that I doubted if enough worshipers would show up to make a service worthwhile.

That did it! I wanted to drop dead! I longed to crawl under the rug! Especially so when my host asked testily, *"Preacher, how many does it take to make a service worthwhile?"*

No whipping administered me in my young years ever stung like that! And none was ever more deserved.

The shepherd in Jesus' parable (Luke 15) was not content when but one sheep remained unaccounted for. And I, the shepherd of the flock entrusted to me, was suggesting that all who braved the elements that soppy winter evening would be expected to provide their own spiritual bread.

Suppose our Lord had been as egocentric as I. Every one of His sheep would have been left to save himself--an impossibility, of course.

And just suppose that on that cheerless evening far back in the country in that tiny church (incidentally named New Hope) had come one seeking salvation, prepared then and possibly only then to dedicate his life to Jesus.

Nine worshipers braved the elements. Nine sang Gospel hymns, joined in prayer, gave ear to the delivery of God's Word, and departed into the cheerless night with an assurance of God's Presence.

How many make "enough"? Just as many as hunger for His blessing--that's how many!

The Christmas I Fed an Army

(Mable)

"I just don't know, honey," I confessed to Edwin. "I'm not sure I want to do it." At the time, we were serving the church we had established in northern Alaska, 120 frigid miles from the Arctic Circle.

Our church had grown into a spiritual haven for a host of townspeople, but also it was ministering to a vast number of military personnel. Many of the young men in service were single-- and faithful to our church, I must add. It never seemed to occur to them to skip a worship service simply because it was a mere fifty below zero!

Now it was early December, winter had set in, and Edwin was seeking my approval before announcing from the pulpit that we were inviting all single men, military and civilian, into our home for a sumptuous repast--and on Christmas Day at that! It didn't require a lot of savvy for me to realize such an invitation would be positively mouth-watering to homesick young fellows.

Yet, I reasoned--could it have been a sop to conscience?--Christmas is for families and who wants to entertain a houseful of single young bucks on that Day? It would be super just to lounge about in robe and slippers, catering to the wishes of the children. Then, I came up with another log to throw on my fire of demurral. Hadn't we made sacrifices beyond number just coming to minister in this ice box?

"It's like this," I explained to my dear spouse as though he had no mind of his own, "it's not a question of the men going hungry, especially those on the military base. They'll have a great meal."

"A good meal, no question about it," Edwin replied "but being served Christmas dinner in a mess hall is a far cry from being in a Christian home for the day."

I knew very well my logical husband had a point. And I really had no objections to cooking for a bunch of lonely men. I love to cook and Edwin is always buttering me up. But I was just not sold on the idea of giving up that one day I cherished for my family.

BUT--I acceded and for the next three Sundays Edwin made his announcement. All single men attending our church were invited to spend Christmas Day in our home.

In December in the Far North the sun skims lazily along the southern horizon, limiting daylight to a few precious hours. One afternoon at 2:30 I observed the first star in the sky. But neither darkness nor extreme cold alters arctic living. Certainly, on this particular Christmas absolutely nothing obstructed the path to our door.

By 11 o'clock the first brigade had showed up--perhaps half a dozen in this contingent. Those mile-wide grins just melted my heart. As each stepped inside he drew a deep, satisfying breath as he was greeted by the tantalizing aroma of roasting turkey.

Other guests were not far behind. Before the clock struck 12 noon, 20 single men--all but two or three from the military base--had converged upon our home, reminding me for all the world of Grand Central Station! David, eight, and Evelyn, six, had long ago put to rest all bashfulness as they considered it their duty to entertain our guests.

Evelyn's shiny red bicycle--many months away from a trial run out-of-doors was still a boxed maze of wheels, fenders, nuts, and bolts awaiting assemblage. And David's new Lionel train sat begging for a bit of track. It was not long before the train was roaring about the Christmas tree. I'm sure it made no less than a thousand circuits with an equal number of whistle blowings. I just knew I'd hear trains chugging and blowing--in my sleep --all night long!

Our guests, who tomorrow would once again be skilled mechanics, trained with Uncle's most sophisticated technology, were now small boys sprawled across the rug, some sorting out bolts and nuts for the bike, others laying out train track and accessories. Half a dozen adjourned to a corner of the room, hoping to become big time financiers at the Monopoly board.

And that's when a couple of tears emerged from my eyes! I just couldn't help it. I wouldn't have swapped that scene for all the gold in Alaska!

With my piping hot dinner now ready for serving, we settled a sturdy piece of plywood across saw horses, over which I spread a couple of my new Christmas cloths. And, presto! Our festive-looking table was as beautiful as anybody's!

It was a cozy fit but by sitting "elbow-to-elbow" everyone was in knife-and-fork range of the table. Edwin invited our guests to express their gratitude--not to us of course but to God. Again the tears welled up as half of the men vied for a chance to be heard. When one young fellow contrasted our table with "the mess hall" I thought sure the others were going to throw him out! The children thought it was hilarious.

With this behind us and grace having been offered, our guests dove in. I thought of what the Lord Jesus said long ago, "...I was hungry and you gave me meat..." (Matthew 25:35). I searched each face at the table and I thought, *This is my family, at least for today.* How could I have ever considered doing anything other than this? I asked myself as platter upon platter emptied under the assault.

Late in the meal when plates were empty and young bodies were full, our David announced, "I can still chew but I can't swallow!" What our family did that Christmas Day would be remembered longer by far than had I pressed for my own way.

As twilight settled in, our guests were oblivious of time. There was still the erector set to challenge the engineers as they concocted outlandish creations. And of course the Lionel still lacked all the accessories to be stationed about the track. Not to forget, more swanky hotels yet to be dickered for along Park Place and Boardwalk.

Long after the winter sun had given way to night, our guests––to the last man––discovered they had room for turkey sandwiches, hot chocolate, and fruitcake. Our children had had the time of their young lives as they had entertained their new pals in their own inimitable way.

When, finally, just the four of us remained to hold hands as we sat about the Christmas tree, our youngest voiced her feelings: "That was the fun–est day I've ever had!" And David, not to be outdone, came up with his bit: "Let's do it again next year!"

"I'm for that!" I agreed. And, strangely, I found I must keep blinking my eyes as I gathered my precious little chicks into my arms, then sent them scurrying off to bed.

Amen! to That!

(Mable)

After Edwin had preached that Sunday morning, we began driving about the city of St. Petersburg––Florida's Sunshine City––in a futile attempt to locate Luby's Cafeteria. It was "somewhere" on the north side where we were to make up a party for lunch.

It seemed to me we'd passed the same old landmarks so many times they were becoming old friends.

"That's the third time I've seen that crummy old building," I announced. "And this is the sixth time I've waved to that little girl in the swing."

I suggested to my brother who was at the wheel that we pull over and ask directions. Seeing an elderly man nonchalantly consuming a tangerine out in his yard, we drew up to the curbing. As he approached the gentleman, my brother got right to the point: "Sir, I'm lost!"

Came back the reply: "Then, son, what you need is the *Lord!*"

The Big Wind

(Edwin)

Immediately after my graduation from seminary, I joined my denomination's Florida Conference and was assigned to a church in St. Petersburg.

On my first Sunday in the pulpit, sixty–five worshipers came out to hear their new preacher. Evidently, it was a masterful message for on the second Sunday, after hearing me preach but one time, the congregation zoomed from *sixty-five*--would you believe it?--to *eleven!* And that's a fact!

Mable's postscript: My dear spouse is telling it as it was, although I'm led to get him off the hook. A big wind may have been blowing in the pulpit but a bigger one was in full effect outside. A tropical hurricane was blowing directly overhead. And there you have a combination of two big winds!

"Whatever Happened to Yellow Boy?"

(Edwin)

Nothing is as scorching as a pulpit in rural Georgia on an August morning! Air conditioning? What's that?

Following worship services in our small church, Mable and I were invited guests of our parishioners for Sunday dinner. Some of the rural homes were without running water, so it's hardly surprising that there were occasions when I scudded to the well just as quickly as decent manners allowed.

On a broiling Sunday, as I gulped the final swallow of my third dip of the gourd, a neighbor sauntered up to exchange greetings with my host.

"Say--" he drawled, "whatever happened to Yellow Boy? Haven't seen hide nor hair of him

After preaching that hot August Sunday I'd never been as thirsty in my life!

in some days."

"That fool cat," fumed my host, "I know 'sure as shootin' where I'll find him--right at the bottom of the well. Figure on fishin' him out tomorrow!"

My dear, innocent wife--standing within earshot and finding the situation hilarious--developed a sudden coughing spell and disappeared I knew not where. I simply turned green as the grass at my feet.

You never know what'll happen to a preacher!

It Took a Miracle -- Make That *Three!*

(Mable)

It was one of those mornings when anything could happen--and just about everything did!

David, our two-year-old, was into everything. Evelyn was but hours away from making her appearance into the world.

With his nose flattened against the glass in the front door, our little son had spied the neighbor's cat, a daily visitor, strolling up the walk. David cajoled me into letting him join his feline friend out in the yard--and actually I'm sure I was glad to get him from under foot for a while.

It was March--and this was Florida--but it was cold. I consigned my housework to a back burner while I buttoned him into his little overcoat, then sent him out to play. Sometimes I called the cat "Jonathan" because he and our David were like the Biblical twain!

I suppose all of three minutes elapsed before I stuck my head out the door to check on my toddler. He was gone! I looked to my Heavenly Father. Frantically, I called to Him: "Where? Dear God, where is my child?"

And then I knew! It was God's answer: "The creek! Get to the creek! Hurry!" At the edge of the parsonage property and separating it from an unkempt field of sandburs and scraggy palmettos flowed a sluggish little stream.

31

I dashed--if a woman in my condition *could* dash!--across an early-spring green lawn, alternately calling for my child and seeking God's guidance as I implored Him to keep His hand upon my little David.

As though that were not enough for me to contend with, you can well imagine who else entered the scene: the devil of course, chastising me for my negligence. Have you noticed--he's not shy just sly! He always seems perfectly at home as he plants his seeds of deception in the garden of the heart.

An eternity passed before I was able to peer over the embankment into the brackish water. And there my little boy lay! I could have cried a "bushel" of tears--but the moment demanded action, not self-concern. In crisis times, I'm convinced we are endowed with a capacity to handle the "impossible." I was a sight to behold as I maneuvered my ponderous frame into the murky water where my child lay. And let me say right here, if ever I doubted miracles before, I was right in the midst of them now. One! Two! Three!

My tiny tot floated on the water, buoyed up by the little overcoat I had secured about him just moments before. Had the morning been typically warm, I would have lost him in that brackish water.

Then, for some unaccountable reason--you don't suppose it could have been God, do you?-- he tumbled down the embankment into the water, surfacing *face up!* My child was breathing! And, miracle three: the stream which flowed with the authority of a raging torrent after a tropical rain was as still as a back yard pool.

I scooped the limp--but not lifeless!--form

of my child from the water and cradled him in my arms. Clumsily, I hoisted him to solid ground, his little body already turning blue--but God had spared him!   Only the Almighty knows how I scaled the embankment. I often wonder if perhaps He smiled at me as I scrambled out--but no matter. It was a smile of love, I'm sure.

Sunsets and rainbows, seacoasts and snow peaked mountains have a distinctive beauty of their own, but no beauty has matched that of the face of my little boy as his eyes focused on me. And nothing has ever been more tender than the tiny arms encircling my neck. The tears I had held in check now burst forth--and I didn't try to restrain them.

Three miracles from the hand of God, in answer to a mother's prayers! And just maybe I should add a fourth. When our baby Evelyn was born neither she nor I suffered the slightest ill effects.

I'm convinced God's miracles surround us, even though we may be unaware of them. Don't you think so?

In the court of justice
none of us would be
sentenced to salvation.

The Man Who Cast His Shadow

(Edwin)

It's just a little ol' place tucked away on the barren Alaska coast, a remote Eskimo village called Unalakleet and pronounced U–na–la–kleet. You are with the majority if you've never heard of the place.

The land is as rugged as you could find, and largely unproductive. Hostile winds come howling in off an angry Bering Sea. Yet, the tiny community across Norton Sound from Nome is populated by genial Christian people.

I was on board an ancient DC–3 that Sunday morning, bound for Nome where I was to fill a pulpit. Our pilot made a refueling stop on what we supposed was Unalakleet's runway.

Mable and I discovered that the most inspiring sight in the village was found in the least likely place: the cemetery. A God–fearing individual who gave the Lord his all found his way years ago to the small settlement––and there he remained. Axel Karlson, a Swedish missionary, served the community for a score of years.

This noble epitaph is inscribed upon his tombstone:

When he arrived in this village
There was no Christian
When he died
There was no heathen.

I'm confident few outside the village have heard of Axel Karlson and fewer still have visited his grave. Yet this man's shadow was cast over an entire community and I can't get him out of my mind! I find I'm challenged! I look longingly for someone to say about me what was said of Axel Karlson--even if it involves no more than my neighborhood.

The British poet, Wordsworth, wrote: "The best portion of a good man's life:/The nameless, unremembered acts/Of kindness and of love."

We'll not all turn out to be Axel Karlsons, the figure whose shadow still enshrouds a small Eskimo village. Yet, more and more, I hold to the conviction that when God breathed life into us, He sent along a pattern whereby we are to cut the tapestry for daily living. How many of us are employing that pattern in our service to Him?

At times, I can hardly believe the lateness of life's hour! Night is imminent. Perhaps you have experienced the feeling. The Apostle Paul needles me--just as he should--when he asserts: "...now is the accepted time; behold, now is the day of salvation: (II Corinthians 6:2).

I have not come upon a day yet when there was not *something* to be accomplished in the Lord's vineyard. How about you?

The Stranger I Drove to the Saloon

(Mable)

He looked so pathetic I could have cried--well, almost!

A cold rain beat down in torrents, my watch had stopped, making me late as I hastened into town to pick up my husband, and now I was eyeball-to-eyeball with a dilemma: pick up this burly stranger and drive him to town or leave him to "drown" at curb side.

"Lord, what do I do now?" I moaned. Yet, already I knew exactly what I was to do. Stop and offer him a ride--and I knew full well he would not refuse in this weather! After all, hadn't I read during my devotions that very morning Jesus' words: "I was a stranger, and ye took me in" (Matthew 25:35). And these words:

"I was a stranger, and ye took me NOT in" (v. 43). Isn't it just weird how we so often entomb our Lord in the sepulcher of uncertainty! Yet, in those final precious seconds of indecision, I desperately clung to another tack: "Lord, You know I never pick up a stranger--my husband wouldn't approve." (Did you catch that: *Eve* once again putting the finger on *Adam!).* But of course I was being simply namby-pamby. I pulled to a stop and the young man wasted no time crawling into the seat beside me.

"Where to?" I asked as we speculated on

37

the weather.

"The Electric Company," he informed me.

That sounded legitimate. He was going to town to settle up his light bill. But in *this* weather, running the risk of pneumonia, just to pay a bill? Wait a minute, Mable! What am I doing? The electric company is not even downtown!

Then, it struck home. The Electric Company where he was headed and which I had seen only from the outside was a saloon. And here I was helping a young fellow get there!

Well, I decided, I wasn't going to give him a free ride. I had a captive audience and he was going to hear my little spiel. I told him that Jesus could do far more for him than a bottle of booze ever could. I said he might not appreciate my advice right then, but to remember what I had said.

And so--I let him out--at The Electric Company--and maybe he would soon be soused, but I'm convinced it was a God-given opportunity. Had I left him standing knee-deep in that torrent of rain I would have hated myself. I did what I felt led to do. After that, it became God's responsibility.

As I picked up my somewhat damp husband, I found myself voicing the little couplet:

God has no hands but our hands
To do His work today!

The Night "I" Caught the Burglar

(Mable)

What on earth was going on over at the church?

As I raised up in bed and glanced at my Big Ben--exactly three o'clock in the morning--I peered across the street from my upstairs bedroom window. Every light in the spacious education building was blazing. Three o'clock in the morning and it looked for all the world like a carnival had set up shop inside.

I nudged my blissfully sleeping husband. "Honey, wake up! Burglars are ransacking the church!"

I may have overstated it, but nonetheless Edwin was not at all impressed so I tried a different tack. "Sweetheart, there are burglars across the street. Suppose they cart off your pulpit!" Still not with it, my darling spouse mumbled the funniest thing I'm sure I've ever heard him say. He asserted, groggily, "I'll go over and help 'em!"

I was just about to yell, "Fire!" when Edwin finally roused and it dawned on him the impact of what I had been pleading. As he sprang from the bed and donned robe and slippers, I phoned the police who responded immediately. By the time Edwin made his way across the street the police rolled to a stop.

A search of every nook and corner of the

building turned up nothing. Finally, one of the officers came up with an idea. The adjoining sanctuary--as dark as the education building was bright--just might offer a clue. Reaching a hand into the dark building, Edwin flipped on the lights.

No one--absolutely no one-- could have cooked up a plot to match the real life scene about to unfold. In the exact center of the sanctuary--as though it were an apparition--stood a young white male, meticulously attired in white coat, white trousers, and a tie.

If ever there was a "gentleman burglar" here he stood! He offered not the slightest resistance nor did he make any attempt to escape.

Then, what was his motive? The young man assured Edwin and the officers that he was not a thief. He was not drunk nor was he high on drugs. What then? He stated he was just out walking around (at three o'clock in the morning and dressed like Sunday--go--to--meeting!) and he decided that just for a lark he would check out the premises. Locating a door carelessly left unlocked, he began switching on lights and was on his way to more of the same when he was apprehended in the sanctuary.

We pressed no charges. The police agreed to no arrest, and the strangest burglar on earth was sent on his way.

And--oh, yes--it did take Edwin a while to get back to sleep. It took me the rest of the night!

"We Don't *Think* She'd Shoot a Preacher"

(Edwin)

"Reverend, we need a mite of help!"

Two officers from the Fairbanks police department stood that September night at my church study door. Over the past several years I had been forced to call upon them and now it was a switch that they should be calling on *me.* Numerous break-ins at the church, coupled with unbelievably obscene acts of vandalism, had resulted in my becoming acquainted with several members of the force.

But what could a clergyman contribute to a situation that a policeman could not handle? I was soon to learn.

"Reverend," began one of the officers, "we're requesting you to accompany us to a home across town where a woman is off her rocker. She's threatened to use her shotgun to rub out any of us 'dogs' from the police force. Says she'll blow our heads off if we show up at her door. We figure she's standing just inside right now, shotgun in hand. But, er, we don't *think* she'd shoot a preacher!"

I squirmed uneasily in my chair. "Not exactly a tranquil scene, " I opined. "Just how do I fit in?"

"We must disarm the woman, reverend, before somebody gets killed," the officer explained.

"And my job is to persuade her to surrender

the gun?"

"That's about the size of it, reverend."

I reached for my phone and dialed Mable at the parsonage. My prayer warrior would cover me while I was engaged in this precarious mission. I knew she would be upon her knees momentarily.

I accompanied the officers in the patrol car as they further outlined the strategy. They would drop me off half a block from the uninviting little log home. "We'll cover you--as best we can," they assured me. I smiled in spite of the gravity of the occasion. With a bullet through my head I'd need more than cover! Again I smiled. They don't think she'll shoot me, I told myself. We'd soon know!

In a steady, cold drizzle I trudged along the narrow walkway leading to the porch. I drew closer and closer to the life-and-death situation: a berserk woman armed with a shotgun versus a clergyman armed with the Word of the Lord.

Every step, I realized, could be my last. Yet I felt secure with a weapon more powerful than a gun: Mable's prayers--and mine. If God could use me to bring this demented, wretched child of His to lucidity, then I was prepared to be His man. I would willingly pay whatever price was required.

I strode across the few feet of rotting porch, raised a fist, and rapped upon the sagging door.

"Who's there?" The words--coming from just inches inside the door--bristled with authority.

How should I reply? No need to call out my name for that would be meaningless to her. But perhaps the announcement of my profession would strike a chord. The words "clergyman" and "preacher" can somehow cut through the bewilderment of a disconcerted mind. It was my best approach, if not my only one. I replied that I was a local clergyman, all the time praising God I had gotten this far! The next move was hers and I waited through interminable silence.

The poet, Edwin Markham, portrays a Roman soldier guarding the sepulcher following our Lord's burial. The soldier bares his emotions: "The night was long, so long it seemed at last I had grown old and a long life had passed." At this moment I could readily relate to the Roman guard!

An eternity crept by before I heard a slight movement within and the moment of reckoning was at hand. Either she was adjusting the gun preparing to use it on me or she was about to shift the lock.

The rusty bolt slid back into its shaft, the door creaked open, and I stepped inside.

My task from this point on was a breeze. The woman I confronted, perhaps forty years of age and attired in clothing as unkempt as her surroundings, appeared relieved as I claimed her weapon.

When finally I believed my mission was accomplished, I departed the squalid little cabin, conferred briefly with the officers, and returned to my own warm home where Mable awaited me. Her greeting as I pushed open the door was her typical expression of praise, a simple "Hallelujah." I observed a couple of out–of–control tears course down her cheeks.

"Honey," Mable said after we had offered our prayer of thanks to God, "isn't it marvelous how He not only uses His children but protects them in danger! God just had to have someone He could call upon tonight, else that poor demented woman might have committed suicide--or *murder!*

      "And do you know what I thought of?" she continued. "Remember those beautiful closing lines in George Eliot's poem, 'Stradivarius'?"

> *'Tis God gives skill,*
> *But not without men's hands:*
> *He could not make*
> *Antonio Stradivarius' violins*
> *Without Antonio.*

I remembered!

The Tastiest Egg on Earth!

(Mable)

There's just no place *anywhere* like India! It even boasts of its own pungent "aroma"--and that takes some getting used to! Yet some of the dearest people I've ever known make India their home.

Take roly-poly Kumudini, for example. God's jewel has now gone to be with our Lord, and I'm thinking of the reward that must surely be hers. But how I would love to just squeeze that precious servant of His one more time. I know of no one who has labored harder for India's children than Kumudini.

When she was a mere child she renounced her parents' Hindu faith, waived all claim to their extensive wealth when they disowned her, and accepted Jesus as her Lord. Did that take courage! I'm not sure that even some of the Biblical "greats" possessed more.

Nothing ever proved beyond the ability of this dedicated soul, including the care she gave the endless stream of little waifs who beat a path to her door. For years Edwin and I worked, through our organization, to help Kumudini feed her ever-hungry and ever-increasing brood.

Then came the day when we, too, showed up at her door. Our train schedule allowed us less than half a dozen golden hours at her compound. At mid afternoon I was loath to bid Kumudini and the children good-by as we boarded the train for our return trip to Calcutta, perhaps 135 miles. I was sure that train made more stops than starts! And yet I had no complaints. We were the fortunate ones, for almost everyone on board--and that included hundreds of jam-packed travelers-- were forced to stand. We were assigned seats in a small compartment.

Darkness descended before we were halfway back to Calcutta, and I began to dwell on that little sack lunch Kumudini had insisted we take along. For me she had packed an egg and since I had not tasted a hard-boiled egg in ages, my mouth just watered for that succulent treat. Edwin suggested we wait till the halfway point in our journey and I agreed, though with some reluctance. For my husband, Kumudini had fashioned a sandwich, ingredients unknown.

Finally, I decided I could wait no longer and I began unwrapping my prized egg. Before I could lift it to my lips, however, our rolling stock ground to its umpteenth stop. And as it did so I glanced aimlessly out the window. The only lights upon the dilapidated little station came from within our coach. What met my eyes just broke my heart.

In a pathetic little semicircle stood a knot of emaciated humanity--small children so frail you would decide they had not eaten all day and maybe not in several days. Strangely, the lights emanating from our coach seemed to focus upon each gaunt little face.

Then, one small boy, as meek as a lamb but possessed of a bit more temerity than his little friends, edged up to our open window and thrust a bony hand inside. My eyes met his--the sunken but still beautiful dark brown so typical of India's people.

And can you guess what I just knew I had to do--and what I wanted to do? The egg, so tantalizing moments before, now held not the slightest appeal. I'm certain I would have choked on the first bite.

As I breathed a prayer for that dear little chap, I lovingly placed my prized egg into his thin, brown hand. Then, as I watched, he darted away into the night like a frightened fawn. I decided it was the first egg that child had ever seen.

Out of the corner of my eye, I watched my compassionate spouse break up his sandwich, doling out bites as small hands took a cue from their more forward companion.

As though we had declared "Mission accomplished" our train began lumbering from the station. Leaning back in my seat, I allowed my mind to dwell on Jesus' command: "Feed my lambs" (John 21:15). What satisfaction I found in that!

When, finally, I plumped upon my bed in The Great Eastern Hotel, I shared my reflections with my husband. "Honey," I declared, "that was a God-given opportunity! Just one minute later I would have consumed half that egg. And do you know what, I'm not at all hungry. Not in the least!"

Edwin added, "What we shared was so small, yet it was all we had so of course it was all God required of us."

I have come to understand so much more clearly: it's not always the quantity we share as it is the quality of the heart. I had shared one small egg--yet it was all God asked of me.

Next time He may require more but--not to worry--He will be certain I have more to share. And this leads me to conclude: we'd better be ready at all times. It just might be He'll call us to share--today! Physically or spiritually we may reach far more for Him than we ever dreamed possible!

Chicken Is Chicken

(Mable)

Have you heard how all preachers are supposed to love fried chicken--and expect it for dinner every Sunday? Well, who hasn't?

In a rural home where we dined after Edwin preached one Sunday, the table groaned with garden-fresh veggies--all delicious, I must add. But not until we had cleaned up our plates was the meat platter passed: fried chicken, of course. A strange custom, it seemed but who was I to ask why? It reminded me of those comic strip cartoons where the freckled face little boy always knows he must consume his spinach before he's served his ice cream.

Somehow, I was the last one at the table to receive the platter, by now rather thoroughly picked over. I must confess that when I'm a guest in a home I study the offerings, searching for a drumstick because I can identify it and I feel comfortable with it. This time I was too late so I speared a batter-encrusted piece I didn't recognize. Then, I went to work on it.

I was becoming frustrated as I made absolutely no headway when my concerned hostess--bless her--discovered my plight and exclaimed, "O, my dear, you don't want that piece. That's the head!"

She was right! I certainly did not want that

piece! When I thought, *What if I had taken a bite, eyes and all,* I managed to remain at the table--but just barely!

Temptress at My Door

(Edwin)

She was a beautiful woman, no question about it.

Caroline was a wife and mother, and she and her husband and their two young boys attended a church I pastored in Alaska.

The ringing of the front door bell of the parsonage shattered the mid-morning silence. My family was visiting relatives in Florida and I had been alone in the Far North for some while. A hallway led from the front door to my study, then on into the living quarters. Parsonage, study, and church were under one roof--and most of the parishioners were familiar with the layout.

Caroline appeared at my door that morning dressed in impeccable attire--much more apropos of a wedding than an informal morning call on her pastor. As she stepped inside the building it became quite apparent that Caroline had drenched herself with exotic perfume.

I ushered her into my study, whereupon she pulled a folding chair close to my desk--closer than the visit warranted, I was sure. She stated the purpose of her call which was a matter of small consequence.

That disposed of, Caroline's countenance assumed the expression of a temptress. Her eyes took on the look of satanic roguery as they danced with all the allurement at her command. Her mouth affected sensual intrigue.

It was obvious to me why this beguiling siren had come. She was familiar with the pattern of the home, the location of the bedrooms--and perhaps she was now relying upon the loneliness of a man in the Far North.

Yet had I not recently preached to my congregation on the Biblical text, "Greater is he that is in you, than he that is in the world"? (I John 4:4). The words "he that is in the world" refer to Satan who at that moment was employing this attractive woman to sell me his alluring bill of goods. The Apostle Paul refers to Satan as "...the prince of the power of the air" (Ephesians 2:2). And Jesus describes him as "...the prince of this world..." (John 12:31).

Caroline's untimely call and unexpected allurement posed a shock to me, rather than an imperious temptation. Certainly it was no matter for debate on my part. I simply sat waiting for her departure and, chagrined, she bid me good morning, turned the corner of the building, and soon was out of my vision.

She was not, however, out of my mind. Here was a respected wife and mother, prominent in the church I served, and offering herself to the pastor--and in doing so she was willing to shatter my career and perhaps my home.

I wondered if I had been overly naive. If seductions are carried on within the church body, what must be the temptations confronting the secular world? Are there other temptresses much like Caroline going about setting alluring traps? And what are these "Carolines" aspiring to accomplish?

I have concluded it largely boils down to this: Satan is having his day, running roughshod over both Christian and non-Christian when permitted to do so. In order to spare our world from spiritual collapse, every disciple of our Lord must dress as meticulously spiritually as the "Carolines" are physically.

We become properly attired through a careful study of the Scriptures, committing passages to memory to become ammunition when needed. The devil cannot stand up against the Word. We don proper spiritual attire also through faithful participation in the church as well as setting apart time for prayer.

I see our nation, and, yes, our world, as not being beyond redemption. As for tomorrow, who can speak? This we do know: Satan thrives upon his successes. All who love and serve Jesus are obligated to initiate campaigns to starve this dealer in deception.

Maybe we've allowed him too many free meals--at our expense!

Satan knows he has a rival
When he sees us with our Bible.

Who Cares?

(Mable)

I just wanted to turn and bolt from the place!

My stomach churned as though I'd stepped off a roller coaster at the county fair. Yet, at the same time, I experienced an urgency to remain right where I was--and cry.

Edwin and I were in Calcutta using our spiritual dragnet to round up God's emaciated little waifs, placing as many as humanly possible in one of our children's homes--giving each child the chance in life we knew he deserved.

One afternoon we were afforded an opportunity to visit Mother Teresa's Home for the Destitute and the Dying. I was sure it could not possibly be as hot as the morning had been. How naive I was! By mid-afternoon I looked for all the world like I had showered with my clothes on!

Upon our arrival at the Home, Edwin and I were ushered into a dormitory type room filled to capacity with a veritable sea of little mats, wall-to-wall, with but inches between them. Upon each mat lay the emaciated body of a woman, just pencil-thin--not yet dead but death hovered over them.

As I beheld the expressionless faces of these ravaged human beings I gained an immediate perception of the ministry of the faithful band of dedicated workers whose compassion and indefatigable efforts had placed them there.

In a valiant attempt to demonstrate mercy to those for whom society no longer had compassion, Mother Teresa and her intrepid little flock of co-workers (I called them angels of mercy) had dedicated themselves to patrolling the streets of the tawdry metropolis. They had snatched these pitiable women from rat-infested lean-tos, from squalid back alleys, from cardboard shacks--all helplessly awaiting the hand of death. The angels of mercy bore these wasted dregs of humanity to the Home, placing them lovingly upon a mat. Upon their knees they washed open sores, bathed fevered brows, and just generally administered Christ-like compassion as I'd never witnessed it before.

As unobtrusively as humanly possible Edwin and I wove our way from row to row, breathing a constant prayer as we moved along. I must confess my eyes were misty as they looked into the expressionless eyes of those I was sure would be gone by tomorrow's sunrise. Although I simply ached to break down and cry at the panorama stretching before me, at the same time I experienced relief just knowing that every single one of those pathetic women would pass away under a blanket of Christian love at its finest. And though past physical redemption, they were not beyond the saving power of my Lord.

I must explain that this marvelous ministry is not for women alone. A room equally crowded with pitiable men adjoined the women's ward. We watched God's "rescue team" bring in a skeletal being, a male whom I judged was well along in years--yet who can know? Starvation hastens the aging process as few things do. We watched the angels of mercy bathe this recent arrival (for decency's sake the loincloth he was wearing remained in place), and I whispered to Edwin that no doubt it was the first time in ages that clean, soothing water had touched the shriveled skin which now resembled parchment.

Before departing the Home, Edwin and I paused momentarily to peer through a sheer curtain into an anterior room where four bodies lay upon a raised slab. In that oppressive heat, I knew death had been recent for a body could not remain there long. When I discovered one was that of a small boy perhaps at the precious age of 12 years, I just boohooed. I couldn't help it. At the time in life when American boys are tossing footballs, shagging fly balls, or working up enormous appetites at the school gym, here lay a child of India dead from starvation. Yet, I felt certain those tireless angels of mercy had been there to comfort him as he breathed his last.

During our two-week stay in India, my husband and I were offered numberless opportunities to observe the sordid side of that boundless country: the feculent back alleys (we visited 20 persons living in quarters that an American couple would have considered much too small), the dung-smeared walls of village huts, the copious rice paddies offering employment with recompense at thirteen cents a day--and in relentless heat.

Often, during those days I found my mind crossing oceans to my own country's shores, and I envisioned with shame my nation's rich farmlands bearing crops plowed back into the ground, meat producing animals shot and bulldozed into the earth, millions of acres of fertile soil lying fallow-- all under the reprehensible guise of "bolstering the economy."

It was then that I longed for every American to trudge the teeming streets of India's cities, to observe just a few of the tens of thousands who sleep nightly on concrete sidewalks, to breathe in the odors singular to India. Perhaps then and only then would our nation cease its flagrant misappropriation of God's bounty.

And just possibly we then will no longer be in urgent need of God's angels of mercy. I have a feeling that a host of improvements just might begin with me!

The Strange Story of Malcolm, the Hitchhiker

(Mable)

If there's anything that surpasses homemade chocolate chip cookies, my dear husband is certain it's yet to be invented!

It was late in the day when Edwin plunked himself into an overstuffed chair (I was sure *he* was about to become overstuffed, too!), armed with a plentiful supply of his beloved cookies. They had been specially made for us earlier in the day by loving friends before we left their home in Miami. Now we were signed in at a motel on Interstate 95, up Florida's east coast, at Titusville.
That evening we were to speak at a church in nearby Palm Bay, but with leisure time on his hands, Edwin decided he should become physically fortified.

Our motel was but a stone's throw from the Interstate, and having a second floor room we were afforded an unobstructed view of the ceaseless flow of traffic.

I was engaged in selecting a dress for the evening. While traveling, I find it often boils down to the *least wrinkled* I have along!

Glancing aimlessly out the picture window toward I-95--at the same time munching his cookies--Edwin's eyes lighted upon a disheveled young chap hobbling about on the shoulders of the ramp leading up to the thoroughfare. My husband beckoned me to his side and we watched mutely as the bedraggled youth lowered himself, tortuously, into a sitting position. This was accomplished by employing the crutch under his right arm as a means of support and making a 360-degree turn as he settled upon the shoulder of the ramp. I suspected it! An empty trouser leg was fastened above the knee. My heart simply ached for him, the epitome of loneliness. Even though he was not *my* son, the mother instinct in me asserted itself and I just longed to hug him, dirt and all!

"O, how I ache for him!" I lamented to my husband. "That dear young man has but one leg," I voiced the obvious as though Edwin would never deduct that for himself. "And do you know, he's about to hitch a ride north!"

It was midwinter and––though mild in Florida––the northern tier of the country had been plagued by bone-chilling cold. And no end was in sight.

"Look how he's dressed!" Edwin exploded. "He'll freeze. I'm going to pray for him right now. Join me?"

Nothing––absolutely nothing––takes priority with me over prayer. Yet, I was seized by a singular feeling––a compulsion––to go to the young man that very instant. When I shared this with Edwin, we bolted for the door. He paused only long enough to snatch a favorite wool shirt from a hanger. I suspected he had no intentions of returning with it.

In order to reach the ramp we discovered we must circumvent a shoulder-high wire fence. The slight detour afforded the young wayfarer an opportunity to size us up as we approached. He had been working on a woebegone little sign--if you could call it a sign. It was actually a jagged bit of brown paper sack upon which he had laboriously lettered his destination: NEW YORK. With the wind whipping off the Atlantic I wondered how on earth he proposed to anchor that tiny bit of information so it could be seen from the highway. Certainly it would never be seen from where he was perched. Furthermore, what motorist, traveling lickety-split up an Interstate would brake to a screeching halt to pick up a disheveled hitchhiker? Add to that the fact that the last weak rays of a winter sun were rapidly fading into dusk.

An infectious grin creased the weathered countenance as the affable young transient greeted us.

"Say!" he began, "you guys don't look the type to be hitchhikers." Then he decided he had it all figured out. "I get it! You spotted me from your motel," and he cast a thumb in that direction.

Edwin nodded as the two shook hands. "So we decided we'd come over and chew the fat for a bit." I confess I breathed a sigh of relief. My dear spouse might have blurted out: "To offer help!"

I'm aware that hitchhikers possess a degree of pride--Edwin taught me this for he rode his thumb in his college days--and while we did come to offer help, both of us recognized the wisdom of a casual approach.

As the three of us bantered light talk back and forth, I decided I was looking into the softest brown eyes I'd ever seen. Without question, here lay his redeeming feature for his auburn beard was scraggly, his long hair stringy. A tan cap several sizes too small jauntily covered the back of his head. He sported a faded blue shirt just lace thin, and I decided it had logged a lot of time on his back. His hands were the color of Everglades muck.

Yet, right here in front of Edwin and me was a child of God, beloved by my Heavenly Father and as precious to Him as any other creature on earth. Fortunately, His love is not meted out according to our physical appearance!

Mentally, I inventoried the young wayfarer's possessions. I was sure that all he owned was upon his back or crammed into a diminutive canvas bag he was using as a cushion. His undersized crutch rested against a thin sapling which seemed to struggle for a foothold on the shoulder of the ramp.

Since I had contributed little to the conversation, I resolved to air my proposals. As I drew breath to speak I searched those captivating brown eyes and with a woman's intuition I knew there was a mother somewhere who loved this young man as I loved my children. How she must hunger for word of his whereabouts, an assurance of his safety, and how she must long to draw him to her breast and plant a kiss on that grimy cheek!

"Young man," I began.

"Name's Malcolm, ma'am," he supplied.

I began again. "Malcolm, night is coming on and I was wondering..." I attempted to sound casual, avoiding even the slightest hint of pity. Yet I honestly could not feel otherwise. I saw him as a young wanderer with little ambition, destitute, permanently handicapped, inadequately clothed, and headed into biting cold.

Somehow, I couldn't quite put together what

I wanted to say--but my husband rescued me. "Tell you what, Malcolm," he interjected as though a tremendous brainstorm had struck him (he loves to ham it up at times--do you suppose all preachers do?), "we have the makings for a couple of mouth-watering sandwiches up in the room. My wife and I will dash up there and slap together something to hit the spot."

I buried my face into the palms of my hands and sighed inwardly. Those *mouth-watering* makings my husband made sound so palatable were peanut butter and grape jelly. Still, if you're hungry and you don't know where your next meal will come from they are not to be spurned. Hours earlier at a rest stop they had certainly hit the spot.

After a moment's reflection (you don't want to appear gluttonous!) Malcolm decided a sandwich or two might very well be just the thing.

While our new friend occupied himself putting finishing touches on his rueful little sign, Edwin and I beat a retreat to our room. I found myself lovingly and even prayerfully digging into the peanut butter jar until it oozed over the bread crusts. Then I applied the jelly.

From the corner of my eye I watched Edwin turn the cookie jar upside down, emptying the entire contents into paper towels. I smiled to myself. *Magnanimous! A real sacrifice,* I thought. But I didn't dare offer a smarty remark!

Only a few precious moments had elapsed since we'd left the ramp. Matter-of-factly, Edwin tossed our wayfarer friend a small, soapy washcloth, and Malcolm went to work scrubbing those grubby hands. After a moment, Edwin slipped him the wool shirt, but this time Malcolm refused what we offered. In protest he threw up a hand, now a blushing pink.

"Can't use that!" he was adamant. He fondly patted the canvas bag serving as his cushion. "All I need is right in here!"

"But all the way to New York City!" Edwin coaxed.

"North of there," Malcolm corrected. "North of New York City."

We let Malcolm have his way, and with darkness now upon us we bid good-by to the young traveler, praying a blessing upon him, a prayer for a ride where he needed to go. And would you believe it! As we turned to walk away I almost blew it! I was about to blurt out, "And, Malcolm, if you're here in the morning...." But then I caught myself and gave myself a mental dressing-down: Mable, you pray for a ride then raise doubts about there being one. What kind of faith is THAT? Yet, the odds were so much against him: it was night and neither he nor his ratty little sign could be seen from the Interstate.

Edwin and I closeted ourselves in our snug motel room and began finalizing plans for our evening when we became conscious of a "semi" chugging up the approach ramp. The driver ground his rig to a halt, then moments later gunned his engine and lumbered onto the Interstate.

We looked at one another. What was *that* all about? Were we hearing God's answer to prayer? I outraced Edwin to the window.

Malcolm was gone! The spindly little sapling which had offered support for him and his crutch was silhouetted against the western sky. A crescent moon offered a kindly benediction before dipping below the horizon.

What a sacred moment--one calling for grateful prayer! God seemed so very real, so loving, so dependable. "He hath done all things well" (Mark 7:37). Edwin took my hands into his. Silence reigned lest we shatter the aura of God's love. Then, we prayed, "Thank You, Father, for manifesting Your power. Thank You for the operator of that rig and thank You for watching over him and Malcolm through the long night. Thank You for revealing Your true nature to us--the God Who answers prayer. And Thank You for the unspeakable privilege afforded us to minister under the bonds of love to one of your precious children!"

Lord, remind us of the brevity of life
and help us to heed Your clarion call
into the arena of life, for You have
said, "The harvest truly is plenteous,
but the labourers are few."

Muktuk or Mukluk?

(Mable)

There's just no place like the Far North for unheard of "delicacies."

In addition to the more palatable meats such as beef, turkey, and chicken, our family has stuck a fork into moose, bear, buffalo, caribou, seal liver, grouse, ptarmigan, salmon, and whale.

Yes--whale! It's known as muktuk, not to be confused, *please,* with mukluk which is an Eskimo boot. But now that I think about it, I'm not sure which would be harder on the digestion! Then, there's squaw candy. You haven't lived until you've eaten squaw candy, according to Eskimo friends. It *is* delicious! I'll let you in on this: you'll recognize it when I tell you it's smoked salmon.

And, of course, there's Eskimo ice cream. The small child in me still has a craving for ice cream now and then. But *Eskimo* ice cream is "a horse of a different color." It's quite simple to make. Reindeer fat is cut into small pieces and mixed with seal oil, then heated until dissolved. Raisins (blueberries in season) are added, along with fresh snow. Serve. My problem was persuading the mixture to go down--without gagging.

But back to Alaska whales. The massive mammals measure sixty feet and those which show up around Barrow--Alaska's northernmost tip--are black except for the nose. They weigh in at sixty-five *tons!* Frayed ends of baleen, resembling palm tree fronds, act as sieves, enabling the whale to strain out the water but swallow its catch of fish. And do they really blow and spout? Indeed, yes. The "blow hole" is at the top of the head above the eyes.

Engraved in my memory is the noontime Edwin and I invited a carpenter who was working about the parsonage in Anchorage to pause for lunch with us. I must say he came to the table bringing along his appetite for he devoured a sizable portion. Rising from the table to return to his work, he pronounced the meal simply delicious. He called my cooking superb. "And may I ask what kind of meat you served?"

I had to smile. "You may ask," I replied, "but you just may not want to know. That was *bear liver.*"

Strangely enough, we got very little work out of him all afternoon. You don't suppose he got to thinking about that toothsome slice of meat, do you?

Were They Angels?

(Edwin)

My calendar said: mid–August. Yet the bone–chilling mist hanging in the air made me wonder. October––maybe? It would have seemed so.

Earlier in the day I had flown by commercial "hedgehopper" into Valdez, an Alaska port town, to pick up my car which had arrived by steamer from the Lower 48. Now I was on my way home to Fairbanks, traveling alone.

Alaska at that time was frontier and living conditions were harsh. Settlements along the road were few and far between and I covered many a mile without chancing upon the first sign of civilization. As for road conditions: the one I traveled was a major disaster.

Washouts were more plentiful than bridges. At mid–afternoon I challenged a washout which was just a bit more formidable than the previous ones––and I more than met my match. The wheels of my car became locked in gumbo, and I could hardly have chosen a more desolate spot.

I revved the engine forward. Nothing gave. I gunned it into reverse. The viselike hold was not about to yield. I was in big trouble and I knew it.

Laying my predicament in the lap of the Lord, I pleaded my case. "Lord, what do I do now?" Jesus' promise, made just prior to the

Ascension, flashed into my mind: "...lo, I am with you alway, even unto the end of the world" (Matthew 28:20). I smiled in spite of my precarious situation for right then it did indeed seem like the end of the world! I might remain locked in the quagmire for hours, possibly overnight, and there were indications it would be a cold one.

Yet, hadn't God promised, "I will never leave thee, nor forsake thee"? (Hebrews 13:5). And the Apostle Paul gave this assurance through his letter to the Philippians, "But my God shall supply all your need..." (4:19).

True to His Word, God had readied a blueprint for my release--and seldom has a prayer been answered more promptly.

Less than twenty feet from my car, to my left and nestled among the birches, rested an Alaska Road Department caterpillar. On top of the big cat lounged two young men in military uniforms. Could this be a delusion, akin to that occurring in the desert: an "oasis" that is but illusory? Not at all! This was for real! But how?

Where had the young men come from? They had no means of transportation. I recall nothing either soldier said, but eternally engraved upon my mind is what they did!

Both sprang into action. After a short search, one located the starter crank stashed away inside the cat, and in moments the rousing of the machine to action was like music from heaven. I felt a grudging release of the wheels from the quagmire as the cat, now behind my car, propelled me to solid ground.

The machine now back in place, the GI's climbed in with me and I drove them "up the road."

After I had released them, I thanked God for his mysterious ways. How else could I account for what had happened except to conclude it was His miracle?

And as for identifying my young liberators, I remain convinced they were angels sent by God. Are you with me?

Contention in the Church

(Mable)

Nobody attended church services more faithfully than Boots!

It was during my husband's seminary days and Edwin preached on Sunday afternoons in a small rural church. We almost met ourselves coming and going that year as he served four congregations.

Having put away a sumptuous Sunday dinner, Boots would amble over from across the road to the church just before time for services to begin. The darling little Boston bull--as friendly as he was ugly--managed to stretch out by the coal stove where he found warmth and contentment.

By the time Edwin got into his message, the little dog was well into dreamland. As my husband preached, the animal snored. Edwin turned up his volume but so did the little terrier. It became so hilarious that I was certain some of the parishioners showed up just to witness the duel between man and dog. I cast my vote in favor of the dog.

MABLE'S PRAYER: Dear God, give feet to my prayers today and fashion realities from my dreams. In mind's eye I envision tortured flesh among India's hurting people, especially among Your little ones. Turn my efforts into nourishing food and sufficient clothing. May my ways become Your ways and my wishes Your wishes that the Kingdom of God will come upon earth. Amen.

The Wedding That Wasn't

(Edwin)

The wedding was set for three o'clock Sunday afternoon.

Invitations long since had been delivered. Flowers, candles, ferns, and whatever were at the church awaiting placement immediately following morning worship.

At noon on Saturday my phone rang. I was greeted by the doleful voice of the bride-to-be, so perturbed she could hardly share her woes. Had the groom fallen from his horse and broken a leg? Been involved in a car wreck? Lost his wallet? Much worse! It concerned the license. "We can't pick up our license till Monday morning," she wailed. "So what will we do?"

I felt for her. She was truly in a jam. The law will not recognize a marriage without a license. If I should proceed with the ceremony, I had visions of the long arm of the law hauling me off to jail before the setting of the sun.

Then, I hit upon a way out--unheard of but, well--why not!

"Just prior to the ceremony tomorrow afternoon," I explained, "I will announce to the audience that this is not the real thing--come back tomorrow. Then, we'll go right ahead just as rehearsed. But instead of pronouncing you husband-and-wife I'll simply halt the ceremony at that point. You'll turn and proceed down the aisle. *Unwed!*"

The news media learned of "the wedding that wasn't" and cranked out a story. However, on Monday afternoon, license in hand, the knot was officially tied.

And, oh, yes, there is this: following the contrived ceremony on Sunday, the mother of the bride pulled me aside to whisper her promise. "Reverend, I'll keep them apart overnight!"

Perhaps the Lord can use a few zillion honorable people like that!

Surely–He Wouldn't!

(Mable)

Why do people stay home from church?

I thought I'd heard them all, but have you heard the one that a member of our church sprang on us? He informed us somberly that he felt it was his duty to stay home with his dog--a perfectly healthy mutt that roamed the neighborhood.

The member's wife was our church's soloist and, well, you don't suppose he.... Aw, no, he wouldn't do a thing like that! Or would he? I'll never know!

Hurtin' People Are Everywhere!

(Mable)

The jangling of the telephone got Edwin up from the breakfast table early that frosty morning in Anchorage. It brought news of a death.

"Who are the next of kin?" I heard Edwin inquire of the funeral director.

"No relatives?" my minister–husband repeated after the mortician. "You say not a living soul?"

When Edwin returned to the table, note pad in hand, I asked, "Who'll be there?" I was referring, of course, to the funeral service.

"Who knows? Maybe nobody!"

These were frontier days in Alaska and what Edwin predicted came true. Not one sympathizer showed up! At the service, conducted at the grave, a pathetic scene unfolded. The funeral director, the clergyman, and the aged gravedigger––that was all.

Later in the day, I shared my emotions with my husband. "Here was a man who lived out his days––no one knows how many, I suppose––and he didn't have a single friend to pay respects! Not one person to see him lowered into his grave!" I could have cried.

Then and there I made a resolution. I had come to this North Country with my family to help make this frontier country a better place in which to live. But surely I could do more. I began asking my Lord to open more doors for me to minister--especially to the friendless.

Even the young military personnel--many fresh out of basic training--were homesick and lonely, hungering for someone to care.

One thing we knew we were to do: convert our parsonage into a home away from home. The news spread! One afternoon I returned from grocery shopping to discover a young air force man making full use of my kitchen. This, in spite of the fact that no one was home! Sleeves rolled up to his elbows, he appeared as much at ease as though he were at his mothers' back East! He was stirring up a cake--his creation all but ready for the oven.

And in spite of myself, I thought sure I would burst as I stifled a laugh early one morning when I answered a ring at my door. It was *early!* There stood a young man in military uniform, asking incredulously, "*Why* was the front door locked? I couldn't get in!" The poor boy looked positively pathetic.

Since those days, Edwin and I have made our home all over the country. And I've discovered that everywhere there's a hunger and a loneliness in the human breast, satisfied only by someone's assurance: "I care!"

God Himself proclaimed--early in the history of mankind--that it is not good for mankind to be alone (Genesis 2:18).

I'm grateful that long ago He brought me face to face with hurting people. I'm going to continue to meet a need among them as long as I have breath.

Join me?

The Big Splinter

(Edwin)

It could not have boasted a more appropriate name!

The young people in our Fairbanks church christened it "The Big Splinter," and here's how it came about:

Several tedious hours after our car caravan set out from the church parking lot--bound for youth camp some three hundred miles down the highway--we abandoned our cars in favor of a wheezing old truck, engaged to haul us the remaining tortuous miles to the camp. No one would hazard a guess as to how many Alaska winters the ancient vehicle had fought for survival. The flatbed was constructed of rough timber, so beaten up the teenagers had logically begun calling it "The Big Splinter."

Packed in among the other campers and the counselors sat a quiet, attractive Indian girl who was in high favor with her peers.

Alaskans are well aware of the fact that the Indian people in the Far North have little tolerance against infection and disease, and when our young girl jammed a splinter off the truck into her hand we should have considered it a warning. Long before the next morning's revellle roused our horde of humanity, we had admitted her into the nearest hospital. Ugly red streaks, an indication of blood poisoning, ran menacingly up the youngster's arm.

When finally she returned to camp amid a chorus of cheers, she had forfeited most all of the week's fun. Lack of attention on the part of the staff had exacted a price.

Almost at the same time, within our church, a member's father passed away. The man lived some distance away and Lennie, for reasons unknown to me, expressed her loathing for him. I therefore decided it best not to call. Lennie was furious. She and her husband withdrew from the church, never to return.

Of course, I was in the wrong. I'm now aware that my neglect brought on blood poisoning of the soul to Lennie. Just as a small amount of attention would have averted a painful experience to our Indian girl, so a consoling visit into Lennie's home would have prevented an anguished spirit within her.

I learned my lesson: neglect of a hurt, whether to spirit as with Lennie, or to body as with the young camper, can lead to dire consequences. A splinter can create irreparable harm, bringing on crises in life. Knowing how to deal with them is a Christian's responsibility. Neglect can promote festering wounds while prompt attention to the hurts of others may prevent further "infection." Besides, it will cause the Kingdom of Heaven to rejoice!

My Cotton Candy Faith

(Mable)

There she lay--brought to her knees by the ravages of fire.

The queenly old mansion which had taken to her bosom many a parsonage family through the years now lay conquered, a blackened hulk of charred ruins. It was a ghastly sight that caused uncontrolled goose bumps to cover my body.

Even before I had rummaged in a dispirited manner through the ashes, I allowed my heart to enter the winsome old dwelling, seeing it as it used to be: in mind's eye I caressed my cherished keepsakes. Gone forever were the treasures dearest to me. Could I ever again go about picking up the fragmented pieces of my life?

And yet, as I began spending more and more time with God's Word, I discovered the admonitions of my Lord washed over me like a tidal wave. Was He really pointing at *me?* Surely not me! Didn't I have every reason to be morose, my treasures gone up in smoke? I was slow to admit it, but no, I did not possess that right!

I was sure my Lord was talking to me every time I read His admonition: "Lay not up for yourselves treasures upon earth,...But lay up for yourselves treasures in heaven,..." (Matthew 6:19, 20). And the Apostle Paul did absolutely nothing for my comfort with his charge: "Set your affection on things above, not on things on the earth" (Colossians 3:2).

So--I began where I knew I *had* to begin--right in my own heart. I began some soul-searching and I decided I agreed with George Matherson, the blind Scottish preacher, when he confessed he had thanked God a thousand times for His roses, "but never once for my thorns." Isn't that the way it is with all of us? I finally was ready to admit that my earthly possessions had been possessing me, while my spiritual treasures were languishing on a back burner. Jesus affirmed that neither moth nor rust nor thieves can destroy things spiritual. And I added my own findings: Nor can fire!

Recently, a friend handed me a cartoon. It depicted four of those ludicrous cartoon-type characters familiar to all of us, and each was either holding his sides or rollicking on the floor, simply convulsed over something hilarious. The caption read: "The devil said WHAT?" Well, what *does* he say? He employs a subtlety and every variety of craftiness ever known in order to sell us a bill of goods which claims that our security and happiness are based on material accrual: the more we have the happier we'll be. But haven't we swallowed--hook, line and sinker--that old wheeze much too long?

More and more, I now pattern my life after Jesus. Our Lord went again and again to the Father for guidance. Early in Mark's Gospel, we read: "And in the morning, rising a great while before day, he went out, and departed into a solitary place, and there prayed" (1:35).

And don't you just love the Garden of

Gethsemane? I can't go there in mind's eye without envisioning Jesus kneeling in prayer. His Presence makes the place so sacred. Mark tells us that prior to the Crucifixion, Jesus instructed His disciples to wait while He went into the Garden to pray, (14:32).

Believe me when I say there's a world of difference between the never failing security which rests in God and the cotton candy claims offered by Satan.

Let me confess: I have lots more growing up ahead. But I now am on solid footing when I say the material things we think we can't live without are largely inconsequential. It was a hard lesson for me but I think I've learned it well!

Nothing is gained through making
bedfellows of yesterday's failures any
more than wooing the companionship
of tomorrow's concerns.

Treasure in My Pocket

(Edwin)

It's just a little book--like ten thousand others--and yet it's unlike any ever published.

The pocket-size New Testament, with a cover so brittle it must be handled with utmost care, has accompanied me twice around the globe. The aged little book was a gift to me from my parents, and on the flyleaf my mother had inscribed the date and place of my birth, the date of my christening with water from the River Jordan, and the date I united with the church. Years later, when I was required to produce a birth certificate in order to obtain a passport for overseas travel, the faded record on the flyleaf was accepted by the Bureau of Vital Statistics as one of the "proofs" of my birth.

The little book won its rightful place in my early years and before departing my homeland for overseas travel I saw to it that my small treasure occupied an inner pocket of my coat.

Now we were in Saigon in the interest of destitute children while a furious war raged on all sides of us.

At departure time, Mable sat in the small, almost deserted white building which served as the Saigon airport. I wandered out on an open porch, hopeful that I would discover our Pan-American plane making its approach.

As I stood scanning the skies--the roar of

gunfire a continuous barrage upon my ears--a young Vietnamese boy, perhaps fifteen, strolled up. In broken English he inquired about the little black book I had pulled from an inner pocket.

And then--unmistakably clear--came the Lord's directive: "Give the youth your Bible--right now!" Of course, the Lord could not have meant it. Allow the lad to inspect it and then return it--yes, that's what He meant! I knew the Lord did not understand why I could never part with my little treasure, so silently I explained it to Him: "Lord, this New Testament is a gift from my now deceased parents and it is a cherished possession. It must be kept in the family." That should do it! Instead, the authoritative instruction was repeated: "Give him the book--now!"

The Pan-Am plane had now touched down, and almost immediately was prepared for departure. Paying no further heed to the Lord's directive nor to the young boy, I joined Mable as we hastened aboard, leaving behind us perhaps for all time the beleaguered little country.

Of course, I was guilty of an indisputable case of disobedience. Now--years later--I have no way of assessing the amount of good that small book might have done, how many lives it could have touched, how many souls might have been saved through its pages.

To be sure, I've carried my small Testament into numerous pulpits as the object of my failure, and perhaps there have been those who were touched by my admission, but somehow that doesn't measure up to what might have been.

Jesus knew mankind well for He declared: "For where your treasure is, there will your heart be..." (Matthew 6:21). My little treasure found its way back into my inner pocket at the time it could have become a winner of souls––how many only God knows.

My disobedience has long since been forgiven by my Lord if I am to believe His Word: "...your sins are forgiven you..." (I John 2:12). Yet, how much more would have been achieved had I stayed within His will! Disobedience comes with a price; we are not let off scot-free. Forgiven, yes. But the consequences lie strewn about as though never quite parceled into what might have been.

In the Kingdom of Heaven I may have to account for my actions to a certain young Vietnamese. I trust he will understand. And I just hope he will not ask: "Americans came to save my country physically, why did you not try to save us spiritually?"

I wonder how I will reply.

I went to His tomb in my hour of gloom
    And asked why He willingly died.
I heard Him declare, "Are you still unaware:
    For your sins was I crucified!"

"Martha"--and Her Hot Rolls

(Mable)

I dearly love Martha of Bethany! And I love her gentle sister Mary. But am I more like one than the other--and if so, which?

I had finished speaking to a group of forty church women gathered for an all-day retreat. We had had a perfectly marvelous morning and the Presence of the Lord just enshrouded us.

If you have ever spoken to a group (or simply participated) where you sensed everyone was in accord, then you can relate to me as the session closed for a lunch break. I went through the serving line with the rest of my sisters as I'm one of those persons who hates to be singled out and gets to go first!

When I claimed my place at the table which extended far down the beautifully decorated hall, a middle-aged woman whom I didn't remember having seen before came with her plate and sat opposite me. Our food had been blessed and I was about to take my first bite of the sumptuous repast when she asked me who I was. I explained I had been the speaker during the morning session. That might have thrown some, but this indomitable soul was not in the least embarrassed by her question.

Then, as though she owed me an explanation, she went on, "I just couldn't get here this morning. Just too many things to do!"

"Something pressing?" I asked, simply attempting to make conversation and at the same time manifest an interest in her. I had visions of an ill husband she nursed at home, or the water heater had exploded and flooded the basement--surely something of major consequence had arisen!

As she cut deeply into the butter, she explained, "Everybody in town knows I make delicious hot rolls. I had to stay home all morning and let them rise and then bake them. I was running every which way trying to get them here in time for lunch [when I went through the line neither she nor her rolls had arrived] so you can see why I missed the meeting." As an afterthought she added, "Did I miss much?"

My heart sank. She had made her choice between bread for body and bread for spirit. While all the rest of us had experienced a blessing beyond description, here sat one who had missed it all. Distraction had accompanied her right to the table.

And do you know what I just ached to do? I longed to reach across the table and share with her how the Lord Jesus had dealt so beautifully with Martha of Bethany! Remember--right in Martha's own home--He had admonished her: "Martha, Martha, thou art careful and troubled about many things: But one thing is needful..." (Luke 10:41,42). Jesus said what Martha needed was that which Mary already had, gained by sitting at His feet.

I'm sure you recall the beautiful account of the two sisters and their brother, Lazarus, who made their home in Bethany, just outside

Jerusalem. I like to think that Jesus frequented the home and dined with the family. I can just see gentle Mary sitting at Jesus' feet, not missing a word He said. Martha on the other hand--often considered "the jittery type"--directed her attention to material things and was oblivious to all that Jesus was saying.

Have you ever wondered how many "Marthas" there are in your community? Or in your church? Each is caught up in a quest for material things. I strongly suspect there is something of Martha in every single one of us! I just love Martha. She's so human and I relate to her, but her days must have been spent as we often spend ours: just no time for "that good part" Jesus covets for us.

Let me share with you my reasons why Martha failed to receive from our Lord all that Mary received--and, of course, apply them to our own lives.

Martha took her eyes off Jesus. Have you noticed that it was Martha herself who had invited Him into the family home? When Jesus is invited in He doesn't hesitate to enter. But He doesn't barge in either. The Bible says He knocks, and when we open the door He comes in! Don't you just love His approach?

Yet, inviting Jesus in is but a part of our responsibility. We are to heed what He admonishes us to do--just "soak up" His Word. And here is where Martha stumbled and fell. After inviting our Lord in she got carried away with material things. The "hot rolls" occupied her full attention. And doesn't that sound embarrassingly familiar! I must confess I have certainly been in

Martha's shoes time and again.

How often have we declared, "I just can't find time for early morning devotions" (a *must* if we expect our day to run smoothly). Like Martha, we become "cumbered about much serving." I went to my dictionary for help in understanding the word "cumbered." It means "hindered." Martha was hindered from receiving the Lord's counsel because lesser concerns took priority. The price she paid was frustration.

In our day and time, many of us have taken our eyes off Jesus through the way we spend the Sabbath. We have become a nation of pleasure seekers. I suppose Edwin and I have heard as often as anyone the old cliché about being able to worship on the golf course, at the ol' fishin' hole, or wherever we choose to be--but do you know, so far I haven't been able to substantiate this through Scripture! Then, too, we've found there's a generous sprinkling of worshipers who make it to church but they bring a wagonload of concerns with them. Others help turn the sanctuary into a ball park the few minutes before the worship hour begins.

One Sunday noon a Methodist bishop broke bread in our home and he shared with us the whimsical little story of the two fishermen. In a certain church the organist was giving the prelude everything she had--a mighty rendition that shook the rafters. It was one of those compositions which ends abruptly, and one of the old-timers was heard throughout the sanctuary explaining to his fishing crony, "Well, I fry mine in *lard!*" Certainly, their spiritual eyes were anywhere but on Jesus! What a far cry from God's charge to His people: *"Be still,* and know that I am God" (Psalm 46:10). Like Martha of Bethany, we take our eyes off Jesus. And we pay for it!

Notice, too, that *Martha was quick to blame another for her predicament.* Doesn't that sound awfully familiar? The fault is not our own, of course; it's always that of another! Can't you just hear Martha butting in right while Jesus is teaching, almost blaming Him as she voices her complaint: "Lord, can't You see I'm slaving away in a hot kitchen while Mary just sits there! Make her get up and help me!"

A little character on the comic page of the daily paper, when in sudden trouble, used to defend himself with a blast at his small friend: "Now look what you made me go and do!"

Today I keep pausing to glance out my window at my colorful petunias growing profusely in a rectangular box on our porch. After last evening's gentle rain each flower has taken on a fresh, pure appearance--just the way I long to be in the eyes of my Lord. My white flowers seem whiter and the red ones possess a darker beauty. I'm sure I can take a lesson from them. When I am willing to place blame on self--when it belongs on self--and not on another as did Martha (or on trivia as the sister did at the retreat), I feel as clean as my rain washed flowers. It makes me yearn to spend more time at the feet of Jesus--like Mary.

Further, I discovered this about Martha: *an attitude such as hers hurts others--sometimes even worse than it harms ourselves.* Have you noticed how Martha was unhappy not only over her own circumstances but also over Mary's? Not because her sister had it hard but because she had it so good! Had I been Mary I'm sure I would have been offended.

How often have we felt sorry for ourselves because, by contrast, others were having it so much better? In effect, we are asking Jesus--just as did Martha in her relationship to her sister--to make others miserable, too! And while we are in such a foul mood--grumpy and staging pity parties--there's little room in our heart for Jesus' guidance.

The next time you find yourself unhappy over your circumstances (right now, possibly?) try a different tack before your misery infects another. Tell the Lord you are ready to serve Him--now! Offer Him your life without reservation and you will be amazed at how quickly your attitude changes. Imagine what might have ensued had Martha joined her sister at Jesus' feet. Both would have experienced a blessing. As it was, I strongly suspect neither of them did!

Now, let me offer you this challenge: promise Jesus you'll not allow the bread of materialism to take precedence over bread for the spirit. I must say I sympathize with my sister whose hot rolls kept her from receiving the spiritual food our Lord had prepared for her that day. But just imagine! Had all forty sisters-in-Christ taken their eyes off of Him and been "cumbered about" preparing hot dishes there would have been no meeting--and each would have been the loser.

Let's keep before us the surety that what we do affects ourselves. But it affects others also!

Liquid Sunshine

(Mable)

"It's a beautiful day in Ketchikan!"
Edwin and I were in southeastern Alaska in the little city where 155 inches of precip fall annually. We were there to attend a conference of our denomination--a five-day session--and our host with whom we stayed was a genial, God-fearing soul with age now upon him.

Every morning--*early*--our warm-hearted friend came bounding down the stairs to announce, "It's a *beautiful* morning!" And I'd bolt for the window and peep through the drapes to verify our host's weather report.

But a sunny day in September in Ketchikan is as rare as rain in the desert. Twenty inches during the month is not unusual so I should not have been surprised that it rained every single minute of every single day we were there!

As our host stood delightedly at his front door, allowing the rain to splash onto his face, I thought, *Here is a Christian brother-in-the-Lord who sees beauty while I grumpily don rain gear-- trying to protect what's left of my coiffure--and splash my way to the church.*

I learned a lesson! Since God made the day it had to be beautiful. Suppose there was no rain. I'd doubtlessly be at the head of the line of complainants: Too much sunshine, Lord! When will You send rain, Lord?

Do you suppose we'll ever learn to accept graciously what God sends and say to Him, "Lord, it's a *beautiful* day!"

I'll do it--if you will!

Strangest Prayer Meeting in Town!

(Edwin)

Hong Kong! Forty youngsters on their knees! In an international airport! And Mable and I were much involved! The events leading up to the strangest prayer meeting in town are these:

Our flight from Taiwan on Japan Airlines was scheduled for departure, bound for Hong Kong, at three o'clock in the afternoon. On a nearby runway a Thai plane was revving its engines, also bound for "The Pearl of the Orient."

As our comfortable craft winged its way through cloudless skies we passed the time discussing plans for the evening: a pleasant reunion of friendships with our orphanage superintendents, David and Mary Yen, escapees from communist China. But as I nursed an uneasy feeling that we should be approaching the Hong Kong runway--a narrow finger of land jutting out into the water--the plane made an abrupt about face. We were headed back to Taiwan--but why?

With usual Japanese decorum, our pilot informed us over the intercom that the Thai plane had crashed on the Hong Kong runway, scattering debris and making other landings impossible. The pilot could have added "human carnage" though it was hours later before we learned the full extent of the crash. The following day, in fact.

The sickening, twisted wreckage of the ill-fated plane, the word THAI in huge letters on the severed tail, was a reminder of our own close call. The crumpled steel had yielded eleven bodies, and it was beyond comprehension how anyone could have been pulled out alive. Our hearts ached for the families of the deceased, but at the same time we praised God for our safety. On that journey around the world, in the interest of destitute children, we boarded 22 aircraft--and each one operated on schedule.

When finally we cleared customs, we joined forty impatient little moppets awaiting us. Our boys and girls had laboriously lettered a huge banner of welcome.

I shook my head in disbelief. "Those kids can't speak or write a word of English," I marveled. "Yet there's not a single error in their banner!"

"I think you should sit down and reciprocate --in Chinese," my facetious wife replied.

Far more important than the fervent welcome was the fact that those intrepid youngsters had held *a prayer meeting* the previous day right in the heart of the terminal. They had watched in horror as the Thai plane had catapulted across the runway to become a twisted hulk. And assuming it was the plane we were aboard they immediately turned to the Lord. Envision a prayer meeting in one of the most unlikely places on earth--the air terminal of the city with the greatest population density in the world!

But why *not* a prayer meeting there? Forty recent converts to Christianity knelt on the soiled cement floor, completely oblivious of the milling crowds.

Across the years, Mable and I have shared

this experience again and again with sympathetic audiences and always it has prodded tears from our listeners. We like to uplift our belief that the prayers of little children come from completely uninhibited hearts, and here is a lesson for all: a child, whether singly or in a group of pray–ers, just seems to know beyond doubt that God holds the solution to his problems.

Jesus Himself declared that the way of the child is the door to eternal life. All of us should heed His admonition: "Except ye be converted, and become as little children, ye shall not enter into the kingdom of heaven" (Matthew 18:3).

If You Had to Choose...

(Mable)

It was the most pitiable little church I had ever laid eyes on!

The small clapboard, one-room houses of worship we served while Edwin attended seminary were cathedrals by contrast! Here's how we came upon it:

A tall, gentle-mannered pastor, dark of skin, whom we had met the previous evening, called for us at our hotel in India's teeming metropolis, Madras. We were whisked away by taxi to a nearby village. Incidentally, cabs in India don't use brakes--just horns! Well, not exactly, but I must admit that from my seat in the back of the cab I'm sure I "put on brakes" a thousand times!

Within the hour, the three of us were ringed by a curious but amiable throng of villagers. These people lived in pathetic little hovels hardly as large as a one-car garage--mute evidence of the poverty surrounding us.

Proudly, the band of villagers escorted us to a slightly larger structure we were told was the church. We stepped from brilliant sunshine into the semidarkness of the windowless structure. I just wanted to cry. My heart ached. For a full moment I stood open-mouthed, simply dumfounded by the stark nakedness of the room.

Where were the pews? Or chairs? Or,

surely, benches? Where were the musical instruments? Hymnals? Pulpit? Altar? Sadly, the tiny chapel was devoid of all these which we look upon as "essential" to worship.

The room was completely bare except for this: on a wobbly little table which suggested many a drenching monsoon rain had poured through the sievelike thatch roof stood *a cross*--two rough-hewed sticks fashioned together. But it WAS a cross! And in spite of such a homely scene, the message was unequivocal. Those simple villagers of India--most of whom had never seen the inside of a schoolroom and could not even scrawl their name--worshiped the same Lord and Savior as other Christians around the globe!

My first reaction was one of pity. How could they worship in such a barren atmosphere? I envisioned them on a Sunday morning sitting cross-legged upon the dirt floor, pitching each tune, words committed to memory--but nonetheless all eyes upon the cross, the instrument God required for mankind's redemption.

I thought again, now in a more repentant mood. Who was I to say that the strange little room, adorned only by a rough-hewed cross, lacked qualities for worshiping our Lord?

Suppose you and I were forced to make a choice: we could settle upon the high-steepled Cathedral-on-the-Avenue with its ever-so-restful pews, air conditioning for further comfort, mighty pipe organ, the finest in hymnals, carpeted floors, ornate fixtures--*but minus a cross*. On the other hand, we could choose the tiny structure of India, completely barren *except for the cross*.

Honestly, if you and I were forced into a

choice, where would our loyalty lie? The effectiveness of the cross, no matter how crude in appearance, far outweighs all the finery mankind has placed in his richly embellished sanctuaries. We are not saved by a profusion of extravagance. We are saved only by the Saviour's blood poured out upon the *cross!*

Without the cross, mankind is lost--forever! As the Scottish poetess, Elizabeth Clephane, penned in 1868:

> *Beneath the cross of Jesus*
> *I fain would take my stand.*

That's where I choose to be! How about you?

"Why Ya Whistlin' Thata Way?"

(Edwin)

The day had not gone well. So--with evening at hand--I decided a stroll to the post office just might buoy my spirits.

Approaching the business district, I observed a little shaver peddling papers. And *he* observed me as I passed, all the while whistling a doleful little dirge. In a moment the brazen little fellow overtook me, then blurted out for everyone within a country mile to hear: "Say, mister, is that the best ya can whistle?"

I bristled. Such audacity coming from the young scamp! I was about to give him a piece of my mind when I suddenly realized the brash little imp had a point. Indeed, the tune was wretched-- if it even qualified as a tune! And, no, that was not the best I could whistle. I could do better--much better!

"Nope, son, that's NOT the best I can whistle," I replied. And I proceeded to give him a demonstration. He sucked in his breath.

"Whillikers!" he exploded. "If I could whistle *that* good I sure wouldn't be whistlin' like ya wuz whistlin' just then!"

That kid was right and I must defend him. He didn't ruin my day--he *made* it. After all, God's word admonishes us to use whatever gifts we have and I assume that includes whistling. We read:

"...let him do it as of the ability which God giveth" (I Peter 4:11).

A bit of extra effort on the part of each of us will make a brighter world. Even whistling!

Incidentally, my darling wife never discovered why I returned home with a half dozen evening papers tucked under my arm.

Truer Words Have Never Been Spoken!

(Edwin)

The visiting evangelist had been in the Far North to conduct revival services in one of the Protestant churches. The evening before his scheduled early–morning departure I ran into him at a family restaurant. Intending to wish him well and to learn if all was GO for his flight home, I found my off–the–cuff comment was a far cry from the meaning I had in mind. I asked, "Is this your last meal?"

In a flash he replied, "I certainly hope not!"

Somebody's Always Peekin'

(Mable)

WOW! You surely have to be careful what you do these days!

You never know who's peeking. Edwin and I had this brought home to us when we were halfway around the world--in South Korea.

Always on the lookout for destitute waifs-- and Korea seems to have more than its share-- Edwin and I concluded a busy day by moseying into the dining room of our Seoul hotel. Actually, I was famished and I felt anything even resembling food would be appealing!

Well, *almost* anything! I must confess the soup which our darling little waitress set before us might have been considered suspect. However, always before I partake of food of any kind I make it a point to thank my blessed Lord for His daily provision. And now I decided He wouldn't let this food be anything bordering on poison!

My husband and I had no more than raised our heads after our prayer when our charming, round-faced little Korean waitress began her dash across the spacious dining room. I was sure there was going to be an unearthly crash between her and some other waitress balancing a tray of hot dishes over her head.

Apparently our young friend was bound for our table. But why? Was she bolting over like an

NFL fullback to warn us to duck under the table before a bomb hit? One thing was certain: I didn't have long to wonder!

Breathless, but rejoicing over her discovery and beaming with delight, she blurted out--not the least bit abashed: "You Christian!" Then, she added proudly, "Me Christian, too!"

Well, praise the Lord! Those fleeting seconds Edwin and I spent with bowed heads as we offered our thanks led to a sharing of God's greatest gift: the Christian faith. Rather than being just another couple of American tourists to be served, we were sisters and brother in the Lord. We were bonded together in our Lord's love, a bond--I have discovered--that cuts through language barriers, color of skin, and nationality.

In our hotel room that evening, I turned to Psalm 146. The canticle begins: "Praise ye the Lord. Praise the Lord, O my soul. While I live will I praise the Lord: I will sing praises unto my God while I have any being."

I closed my Bible. "Thank You, Lord," I prayed, "that I didn't flub my God-given opportunity!" We just never know when we are influencing for good or evil.

Remember--someone's always peekin'.

Heaven's Light in Hell's Darkness

(Edwin)

If there is a hell on earth, Mable and I have been there!

> *Prostitutes gawking from behind every cracked door! Chinese opium smokers within touching distance--and threatening to pounce upon us at every turn! A pitiable old crone squatting beside our path, roasting a dog!*

This was Hong Kong, and when I learned of the infamous eight-square-block expanse in the teeming metropolis--an area known as The Walled City--I shared with Mable my intentions: I was going in.

"You're not going into that hell-on-earth dive without me!" she asserted. "If you go, I go! As Ruth declared to Naomi, her mother-in-law, '...whither thou goest, I will go.' * But is it safe--I mean just the two of us, and foreigners at that?"

Of course it was not safe. But we discovered a way open to us. A God-fearing

---

* Ruth 1:16

Chinese couple, David and Mary Yen, agreed to give us a tour.

"You might somehow manage to get in," David affirmed, "but you very likely would come out feet first! Remember, these people have seldom seen an American and they are not overly hospitable to strangers!"

And so in we went. From street level we dropped down a flight of stairs into another world-- an underworld in every sense of the word.

The four of us wove our way through narrow, circuitous corridors where an open sewer, with all of its stench, flowed but inches away. Where it overflowed onto our pathway my feet began slipping out from under me, yet a guardian angel, I suppose, sustained me before I was bathed in slimy filth.

Prostitutes gawked through doors barely cracked open. Opium smokers--mostly withered old men with dulled senses and pathetically hooked on the narcotic--slithered past us. Any temptation to snap their picture was promptly squelched when we were warned they very likely would kill anyone with a camera.

A wizened old woman perched along the path roasting a dog--or if not a dog, then a cat, according to David and Mary. Another, equally pathetic and with parched skin resembling leather, ladled soup, still but inches from the open, feculent sewer. As we pushed on, the corridor in this hell-on-earth seemed to darken with each uncertain step.

Then, suddenly, the incredible! We found ourselves in a small Christian chapel where David and Mary proclaimed the Gospel amid the darkness of sin.

Seldom have I been more moved. My dear spouse gave way to tears of rejoicing. A dauntless couple, unmindful of risk to life and limb, had lighted a candle in spiritual darkness. If ever two servants of our Lord obeyed His entreaty, here they stood. Jesus charged, "Let your light so shine before men,..." (Matthew 5:16).

At that moment I mentally reversed the sands of time to that sacred scene in Bethlehem. All around the Infant Jesus lay a world blanketed by sin and spiritual darkness. In the small hovel back of a crowded inn, God's ineffable Gift began shining in a sinsick world. Now, in an equally sick modern day world I stood beholding a seldom seen devotion of His disciples who determined to keep the Light glowing.

Often have I praised God for His dedicated followers who are satisfied only by becoming lights in the darkness. I'm challenged to turn up my own spiritual wick for I suspect unnumbered "Walled Cities" are all about us. One small light may seem to offer no difference in our darkened world--but each one does!

What's in a Name?

(*Edwin*)

When we assumed the pastorate of a certain church, the congregation decided upon a "surprise" for the new preacher and his spouse. Before our arrival, every parishioner took it upon himself to learn how to pronounce our name which, incidentally, is PUR–VI'–ANCE.

Upon our arrival we discovered what our congregation had so proudly accomplished. Also, we discovered everyone had learned how––not to pronounce our name––but to *mis*pronounce it!

* * *

Two small boys in our church were discussing our name.

One boasted to the other, "I can even spell Purviance!"

"Naaw!" was the reply. "I betcha can't!"

Began the first: "It's P–E–R..."

"I knew it! I knew you couldn't do it," crowed the other. "It's not P–E.... It's P–*U!* Got it? P*uuu!*" I never summoned up the courage to inquire of the lad if he was spelling my name––or describing my sermons. One Sunday, following the benediction, a middle–aged woman in the congregation declared, "Good sermon, Reverend P–uuu!"

Built on Aching Backs

(Mable)

There it stood before us--a masterpiece in marble: *India's Taj Mahal!*

Bathed in early morning sunlight, the Taj sparkled like diamonds. A 17th century project requiring seventeen years for its completion, it is a creation of architectural genius.

As Edwin and I approached the resplendent structure, we were met by a dark-skinned, nattily attired young chap in Western wear, and for a reasonable fee he agreed to serve as our guide. He shared bits of information as he led us down a long, cement walkway, bordered by a profusion of multicolored flowers, and surrounded by beautifully manicured grounds.

When we reached the marble slabs leading up to the interior of the structure, we were directed to remove our shoes. "If they're not here when I get back," I facetiously whispered to my husband, "I'll have to travel a hundred miles in stocking feet!" But all the other tourists were going through the same procedure for we were about to enter a mausoleum where lie the remains of the Mogul Emperor Shah Jahan and his favorite wife. She *should* have been his favorite! We were told the poor soul bore him fourteen children, then died while still in her thirties.

Inlaid in the mausoleum walls are gorgeous

flowers fashioned from precious gems. For example, just one poppy is composed of 32 stones, while one lotus flower has twice that number. I have no idea how many of these priceless little blossoms are imbedded in the walls. I know my heart simply ached when I discovered that unscrupulous thieves had at one time or another chiseled numerous gems from the imbedded designs.

Edwin and I absorbed as much of the splendor as possible then returned to the out-of-doors where we stepped into our shoes. I need not have shown any concern for their welfare (of course, I *really* didn't!), because not only were they right there, but someone had meticulously turned them around so all we needed to do was to step into them. Naturally, it required no "private eye" to locate our benefactor, and I quickly smothered a laugh over the man's antics. A real ham, he feigned absolute astonishment that Edwin would even consider covering his itching palm with a reward!

Earlier that morning we had boarded a tiny hedgehopper of questionable vintage at the New Delhi airport (that's what I meant about my other shoes being a hundred miles away; all of our luggage had been left in our hotel room for the day). The little plane had landed us at Agra where the Taj is located. Let me confess, when late in the day we were back on the New Delhi tarmac I breathed a prayer of thanksgiving! I was not at all sure our plane would remain in one piece!

In our room at the Ashoka Hotel that evening, I voiced my thoughts to my husband. "What we beheld today," I began, "was simply amazing. Right in the midst of incredible poverty and despair stands that magnificent gem, the Taj."

For the next moment I allowed my mind to wander over that vast country where squalor is the rule and not the exception. I recalled the morning we had ridden a bus so far back from any semblance of modern day living that we decided we were the first white Americans the village people had ever seen. I just couldn't refrain from smiling as those dear people gathered around the bus windows to gawk at us, making the operator's task of unloading produce from the roof of the bus a difficult chore. I'm sure he became a bit irate at the people--and at us!

I continued: "Honey, seeing abject poverty just a stone's throw beyond the Taj grounds--in every direction--makes me wonder. What was the real purpose in erecting such a priceless structure? Wasn't it actually for self-glorification? A powerful monarch expended untold wealth and burdened the backs of *two thousand* of his impoverished subjects. I wonder how many of those pathetic peons perished under the load and the merciless heat. When they dropped over dead while serving their taskmaster--as I'm sure scores did--their bodies were tossed like cordwood upon a pyre."

True, the structure is--and long will be--an architectural jewel. Yet, I find I can no longer give credence to the Mogul emperor. The price in human misery far outweighed whatever significance might be attached to a monument erected to an individual.

How much more meritorious would have been the achievement of the sovereign ruler had he invested his limitless fortune in bettering mankind!

Life is so meaningless for those who in any way memorialize self. The Taj will eventually crumble but investments in the welfare of others are eternally secure in the Kingdom of Heaven.

I stand with the Apostle Paul. That gallant follower of our Lord enjoined us: "...whatsoever ye do, do all to the glory of God" (I Corinthians 10:31). How often have we altered Paul's behest to declare "to the glory of *man"!*

Let this never be so with you and me.

God Uses "Little People" Too!

(Edwin)

I spotted him heading my way!

Since we were the only Americans in the crowd it was no big deal for him to locate me. The bright brown eyes, typical of India's citizenry, were focused upon me as he approached.

We stood that humid summer afternoon--Mable and I--on a railroad platform in West Bengal. We had completed a visit with the "rescued" children in our orphanage in Asansol and now we were awaiting transportation back to Calcutta. As everywhere in India, the platform was seething with restless humanity.

He was a lad of nine years, I judged. His right arm was no more than a stump. With an infectious grin, he greeted me in his tongue, Bengali, while I returned his greeting in English. That was the extent of our conversation, but no matter. He was a "businessman" with little time for chatter.

The lad dropped to his knees and proceeded to open a small wooden box he had cradled under the stump of his arm. He was a shoeshine boy--an enterprising little fellow who had refused to accept life lying down. Almost reverently, the child --always bearing a grin--placed my foot on his rough-hewn little box and began applying polish. The shine rag he wound snugly about the shortened arm and raced the rag back and forth with professional artistry. As for the final "pop", he had it down to a science!

I was impressed with his workmanship--and my young friend was equally impressed by my reward for a job well-done, small in my estimation but sizable in his eyes.

As the train to Calcutta chugged to a stop at the station, I waved a fond farewell to the resourceful lad and, tucking his "business" under the stump, he waved until he lost me in the surging crowd.

Times without number I have returned through memory to that jam-packed platform and the nameless little fellow who entered my life so briefly. He'll carry his affliction all his days, yet I'm confident he'll never sell out to defeat.

Wherever he is today, a young man in an overly populated, poverty-stricken country, he will remain an inspiration to me--and perhaps to others.

If *he* can face the world and all it throws at us, why should *I* ever succumb to discouragement? It leads me to take even more stock in the age-old adage: *if he can, I can!* Perhaps you feel that way too.

Left Turn Was the Right Turn!

(Mable)

"Turn left! Turn left! Turn left!"

It was late and freezing cold--a dark November night in Fairbanks where Edwin and I ministered. We were returning to our cozy little parsonage after a lengthy meeting and as we drove north toward Airport Road I received a bizarre directive. I was sure it came from the Lord--no ifs, ands, or buts about it! We were instructed to make a left turn and head west on Airport Road. Why, I had not the slightest notion. And of course the human side of me took charge.

"Lord," I argued, "You know that road's going to be icy and dark and dangerous and..." But do you know, the Lord was not in the least impressed by my puny excuses! So, I then instructed my husband, "Honey, turn left! Quick!"

Edwin was as bewildered as I, but both of us discerned the Hand of the Lord directing us and we knew better than to be disobedient even if I did put up a small argument. Have you noticed that someone must pay a price when there's disobedience? I shudder to think what might have resulted had we in this instance failed our Lord.

Half a mile down Airport Road we detected the ominous wailing of a siren. Red lights were flashing and--as I always do--I simply cringed and glided a bit closer to my husband. "O Lord," I breathed, "not an accident on this frigid night!" But of course it was! The ambulance crew was not just out for coffee!

"At the Gilford home," Edwin declared as we drew near. Martin and Marie Gilford were a black couple, prominent in church and community affairs. They were the parents of four children. Carl, the inquisitive one, was eight. Tina was three.

With the same degree of authority we had been spoken to moments earlier, we were directed to follow the ambulance—immediately!

Due to the road's treacherous condition, we remained some distance behind the ambulance, but we were not long in learning the horrible accident involved the Gilford children.

Mischief-making Carl had succeeded in reaching the top dresser drawer in his parents' bedroom. There, concealed under socks and handkerchiefs, he came upon his father's high-powered revolver. When his inquisitive fingers pulled the trigger, the gun discharged. The bullet splintered the drawer, drilled its way completely through his baby sister's body, and zinged into the wall.

Martin and Marie, along with the surgeon on call, a team of nurses, and Edwin and me, gathered about the operating table, all eyes focused upon that tiny bundle of humanity, her little naked body twitching in anguish. The hideous sight of her intestines protruding from her small body offered a grim reminder that death hovered over the child. Yet, amazingly, the little darling was still conscious!

Each of us bowed to the pathetic request of the distraught father who bade my husband,

"Baptize her, reverend, before she dies!" Loving hands reached out toward the little girl, and utilizing an operating room bowl filled with water, Edwin conducted a *brief* service. As we trudged from the room, my eyes caught those of the surgeon and his look of futility affirmed my fears: the child's life hung by a thread.

"Honey," I whispered to Edwin upon entering the waiting room. "This is going to take an awful lot of prayer!" And through that seemingly endless night our vigil continued. Not until three o'clock in the morning did word come from the bone–tired surgeon: "*Tina will live!*" And THAT was cause for real rejoicing!

But what of Carl? No one had seen him. The terrified youngster had bolted from the house, unprotected against the Arctic cold. Hours later he was found on the steps of the spiritual shelter he had come to love--our church. He was cold, but very much alive.

The years sped by and Edwin and I completed our ministry in the Far North. Tina--like all healthy children--grew to maturity and fell in love. Martin and Marie mailed Edwin a round trip plane fare, with an invitation to return to Fairbanks to perform her marriage ceremony in the church we served. Unfortunately, details could not be finalized for his trip, but it presented Edwin and me one more opportunity to praise God for His miracle.

In memory I've returned to that nocturnal scene uncounted times. Had there not been that insistent TURN LEFT on that bitter November night, would Tina have lived--or died? Who can answer? Yet, I am convinced that the directive from the Lord, the baptism, and the all–night prayer vigil did much to bring the tiny tot through.

If nothing else, my faith in God was vastly strengthened. Let me say it again: I believe in miracles!

My Smashed Ego

(Mable)

If ever I got taken down a peg or two, this was it!

Later, I laughed all the way back to my home in Missoula--but at the time I thought it was anything but funny.

A group of church women had invited me to speak at a noon meeting a hundred miles from home. The distance I did not mind, especially with Edwin along to help with the driving. Besides, I'm much more relaxed when I don't travel out of town alone.

When we arrived a few minutes before the hour we discovered the women were already seated around a couple of tables in the social hall. Edwin and I were left to find seats for ourselves. After a sandwich lunch, the chairperson, a heavyset woman whom I still had not met (almost nothing had been said to us by *anybody),* conducted a small amount of business. Several of the women began thinning the ranks of the already sparse attendance as they tiptoed from the room, not to return.

When the time came for me to speak, I decided the leader would surely stand--something she had not yet done--welcome me, announce my topic, and offer a few remarks she had garnered from the compendium I had sent her.

My ego balloon soon burst. Without rising, without mentioning my name nor my topic, and without a word of greeting, she glanced down the table at me and announced: *"You're on!"*

Rx for Improving Church Attendance

(Edwin)

It's a pretty serious affliction!

It's known as *sabbaticus morbus*—or Sunday sickness—and it just may have invaded your home, ruthlessly attacking members of your family.

Unfortunately, this malady has descended upon parishioners in every church I've served. Symptoms are easily identified.

The attack strikes about mid-morning—Sundays only. Shortly after consuming a hearty breakfast, the victim experiences an exhaustion of such severity he is unable to attend morning worship services.

By noontime the attack has worn off and the indisposed is perfectly capable of consuming a sumptuous Sunday dinner. During the afternoon he evinces no ill effects while on the golf course, at the ball park, or behind the lawn mower.

Toward evening, the attack recurs with such acute distress that the patient is again unable to show up for worship. However, this attack is also short-lived and, once gone, there'll be no further occurrences for a period of seven days, at which time it likely will return at the identical hours as the previous assaults.

PRESCRIPTION FOR CURE: Take one

Bible chapter daily;   chew on the Word till thoroughly digested;   swallow one or more devotions daily;   take frequent walks about neighborhood, pausing at homes of shut-ins; offer small doses of prayer while pausing; carry along ample quantity of pure milk of human kindness, being certain that neighbors are well supplied; keep bread on hand (the spiritual variety), ready to break and share as need arises.

Make date with a Companion to accompany you to church next Sunday: the Lord Jesus. As Great Physician, He is Healer of all afflictions-- even *sabbaticus morbus!*

The Little Boy Who Died--Yet Lived

(Mable)

I just knew something was amiss!

Isn't it simply weird how one can sense the fact that things are going wrong?

Nurses in crisp white uniforms were scurrying about outside my room in St. Joseph's Hospital in Fairbanks. Earlier that morning I had given birth to our third child, a robust little fellow Edwin and I had waited for, longed for, prepared for. But--unable to breathe--Robert Alan was never to be a part of our family. And yet, at the same time, he became very much a part of it.

When sympathetic nurses tiptoed to my bed that March morning, I had already settled the matter with God, satisfied He would steel me for any eventuality. But even so, what greater heartbreak can descend upon a mother than that caused by a walk through the valley of grief, engendered by the loss of her child? My gracious Lord just seemed to reach down, as only He can do, and tenderly gather my little boy into His arms, another jewel to be added to His eternal Kingdom.

I found tremendous comfort in a little verse tucked away in the Old Testament book of Zechariah, a minor prophet, who wrote: "And the streets of the city shall be full of boys and girls playing in the streets thereof " (8:5). The sixth century B.C. sage may have had ancient Jerusalem in mind, but I have accepted his word portrait as a reference to the Kingdom of Heaven. After all, what else would God do with His little ones except grant them a prominent place in glory?

Though he left us with broken hearts, our Robert Alan has through the years--touched in an indirect manner countless thousands of other children around the world.

A decidedly new facet which was to change the course of our lives had its inception one morning when I stood in the narthex of our Fairbanks church. The frigid air of the out-of-doors was barred from icing down the sanctuary by a plain glass window. Small wonder, then, that the idea struck me: what our beloved church in the Far North lacked was a lovely stained glass window-- and we'd place it there in memory of our little son! Goose bumps just covered my flesh as I considered my brainchild, and I could hardly wait to share it with Edwin. What an inspiration such a window would prove to be!

But--not so. The vision I had deemed so perfect was simply peanuts when contrasted with the bombshell my Lord was about to spring upon us. When He unfolded His plan, we tossed the idea of the window completely aside. God was about to use us to touch souls, and while we would have been doing this on a smaller scale, His blueprint excelled anything we could ever have conceived of! His message was crystal clear and so perfectly unfolded that it offered few loopholes for declension. *We were to establish--in our baby's memory--a charitable corporation to feed, clothe, teach, and love starving little waifs across the seas.*

I couldn't believe it! Why us, Lord? We confessed to having had no training whatever in such work. Yet, have you noticed it's been this way throughout history? Again and again, God has reached down and laid His hand upon some of the least qualified to do His special work. Think of the disciples--not a polished attorney nor a creditable banker among them! Consider Simon Peter and Paul and young David and Moses the graybeard-- how many of us would have chosen even one of them? I'm sure I would not! But God knew exactly whom He wanted, and where, every time.

Left to my husband and me, God's project would never have flown, but as the Lord assured Paul, He assures us all: "My grace is sufficient..." (II Corinthians 12:9).

In quest of destitute children, we boarded and departed 22 different aircraft--some overseas I was positive were held together with baling wire and chewing gum. As we alighted, I confessed more than once to my husband: "Honey, I never did put all my weight down in that thing!"

Edwin and I soon discovered you simply can't tour India, Korea, Hong Kong, the Philippines without departing with a crushed spirit. We found the children, as thick as leaves in autumn, emaciated, half-naked, buried in despair, and certainly not ever having heard the glad good news of salvation.

The financial help we were dependent upon came from all over. These people were our sponsors, and they agreed to support the children we had rooted out from India's squalid back alleys, Hong Kong's Walled City (we dubbed "the den of sin"), and Korea's park benches and moving trains where hundreds are abandoned.

We placed our precious little waifs in substantial structures--not exactly the Waldorf-Astoria--but a mile above anything they ever knew existed. Talk about a new life! *World's Children, Inc.* reaching thousands of youngsters, all in our little son's memory!

A stained glass window--surely a thing of indescribable beauty! But a stained glass, in spite of its splendor, cannot quell the hurt in a small child's heart. In his own inimitable way our special little person continues to bring comfort to Edwin and me--and to that vast host of little moppets God has permitted us to bless in His Name.

I have just read Matthew's Gospel, and these words of Jesus remain inscribed in my memory: "Inasmuch as ye have done it unto one of the least....ye have done it unto me" (25:40).

Bullets from a Bawdy House

(Mable)

I've never been so scared in my whole life-- and, I suppose, never any closer to death!

Shots from a high-powered rifle were zinging around me almost faster than I could count. I felt like Clara Barton and Florence Nightingale rolled into one--although I'm sure not as brave.

Bedtime for our two small children was at hand and the three of us were trudging up the stairs to our apartment in the church in Anchorage. Always bouncy as a rubber ball, four-year-old David pranced from the top step down the hallway to his room. Seconds behind him I came carrying two-year-old Evelyn in my arms.

And that's when the shots erupted! The first bullet plowed through the outside wall as though it were made of tissue paper. Hardly slowed, it whined across the hall, burrowing into the wainscoting three feet above the floor. My little son had escaped by a whisker! "Lord," I breathed, "how great thou art!"

But I was not yet out of the woods. Another shot tore into a window casing, followed by a third which crashed into the floor near my feet.

Next thing I can recall I had slung my babies under a bed--not necessarily the safest place, but who can think when you can almost smell death at your door?

Other shots followed--four, I'm certain. But they sailed harmlessly over the roof--if there is such a thing as a "harmless" shot aimed at your home with you and your precious flock inside!

When finally I concluded my home was no longer a battleground, I gathered up my little chicks and tucked each into bed. Again, I praised God that His hand had preserved us.

After Edwin returned home from his pastoral calling and my heart again approximated normal, we surveyed the damage to our home--inside and out.

"I'm no Sherlock Holmes," Edwin opined, "but it doesn't take a sleuth to determine those shots came from over there," and he gestured toward a small house across an undeveloped field. The place was a bawdy house, as the whole city knew. "Customers" beat a path to the door day and night.

We decided a tipsy young buck, standing in the bawdy house yard, had chosen our home, the parsonage, for a bit of target practice. And he had almost scored a bull's-eye!

Days passed, then one evening after dinner who stood knocking upon my door but the madam herself! My knees turned to rubber. But somehow I ushered her in. She was a middle-aged, squatty little thing, shoulders stooped, her face hard yet remorseful. I felt for her for she was beyond doubt as uncomfortable as I would have been had I entered her quarters! She had screwed up a bucket of courage to make that visit and I respected her for that. After all, I had never had the backbone to visit *her* in the Name of the Lord.

I told her I was glad we could get

acquainted. I explained we certainly had no intentions of pressing charges over the incident, that the Lord's way is always to forgive and since I serve Him I was not vindictive. Even though I may have had every right to blister her, I knew that as a Christian I really didn't. What would Jesus have done? Hadn't I ventured into this frontier town to help? Certainly not to crucify anyone.

I don't know that I did all I could--or should. Yet, would you believe it! Sometime later the bawdy house closed! To God be the glory!

The Lord knows I muff many opportunities He gives me. But I'm grateful that "honey" prevailed over "vinegar".

THE GOSPEL ACCORDING TO MARY

How aches my heart to think the world rejected
      Him!
How oft, upon my knees, have I lifted heavy hands
To God, His true Father!
Is God's heart as breached as mine?
What balm is there for me? 'Tis this:
When all the world acclaims Him
"The way, the truth, the life,"
My soul shall then be bathed in peace,
And in the Eternal Kingdom
The gathered saints shall call me blessed among
      women.

Prayer in a *Rest Room?* Well, Why Not?

(Mable)

Let me say it right here and now: I've not always been the obedient servant of my Lord you might think I have.

For instance, there's the painful experience--as vivid as an unpleasant dream--carved into my memory that Saturday night in Fort Collins, Colorado, where Edwin and I were attending a dinner. The dining hall was packed.

In the interval between the meal and the program I headed for the rest room to freshen up. When I pushed open the door, I was sure the place was on fire. *Why doesn't somebody grab a fire extinguisher?* I thought.

Then, in a voice so soft it reminded me of a mother stilling her child, a sister in the Lord seeing my indecision urged, "Come on in, honey, and excuse this awful smoke. I'm the cause of it. I just can't break the habit, and I desperately need *someone* to pray for me!"

WOW! Talk about fields being white unto harvest, as God's Word says! One of His precious children, enslaved by a habit she apparently could not break, stood begging for prayer to help her conquer the cigarette habit. And there I was, a prayer warrior--I THOUGHT!--offering her not the slightest bit of encouragement.

Instead, I listened to Satan whose presence was much in evidence: "Not in a *rest room,* of all places," he admonished. "Anybody coming in will think you are a couple of nuts!"

And so I cast my allegiance to Satan. I replied to my pitiable sister, "Yes, after the meeting you should get someone to pray for you." Seconds later she was gone and as I watched her disappear my whole being just crumbled. I identified with Eve in the Garden. I, too, had disobeyed my Lord. Never again was I to see this hurting sister for she was quickly swallowed up by the huge crowd.

What an opportunity God had offered me! How wide He had opened the door! Prayer in a rest room? Why not? What better place--if that's where the need is?

Do you see how imperative it is that we be prepared to act *now?* I continue to grieve over my failure to help my sister--and my Lord. She had the courage to admit her weakness. I lacked the courage to minister to her need.

Where is she today? I've often wondered. Her habit which I might have helped her overcome may have dug for her an early grave. I simply did not have on the spiritual clothing the Apostle Paul exhorts us to wear at all times: "Put on the whole armour of God, that ye may be able to stand against the wiles [i.e., enticements] of the devil" (Ephesians 6:11). *

Because I was not properly dressed spiritually I lost my chance.

---

* I suggest you read Paul's full instructions: Eph. 6:11–18.

Running on Empty

(Edwin)

It was a festive occasion and excitement ran high.

A wedding was about to be held in a tiny community in interior Alaska. Such occasions are few and far between and when one does occur, "everybody" shows up--and in a jovial frame of mind.

The starry-eyed groom pledged his faith to his blushing bride and she gave her promise to him. Well-wishers crowded about the blissful young couple, each awaiting a turn for hugs and kisses.

I had flown that mid-March morning in a single engine "four-seater" from Fairbanks, perhaps a hundred and fifty miles away, to the well-kept Civil Aeronautics Administration community called Lake Minchumina. At noon, in the spacious home of the bride, I performed the ceremony.

Now, hours later and the festivities behind us, the entire community promenaded to the little ski-equipped plane waiting to fly the newlyweds, the best man, and me to Fairbanks.

Seated directly behind the bridegroom who piloted our "hedge-hopper" I gave a cursory glance at the gasoline gauge: exactly on half. Since half a tank had brought the three of us down, it was logical to assume a half tank should get us home.

Or would it? Who has not noticed how the last half in an automobile is guzzled down as though the thing had sprung a leak? And now our load was greater. There were four of us--and luggage.

The tiny craft roared from the snow packed field into the late afternoon skies and an uneventful hour passed.

Just as the beacon from the Fairbanks tower--still miles away--swung into view, the engine sputtered, caught up valiantly, then coughed its last. Our fuel tank was as dry as my throat at that moment as we began our descent from 3,000 feet toward a merciless expanse of hostile wasteland. A network of scrubby evergreens, interspersed with spruce and birch trees, extended as far as the eye could see.

The ever-present words of the psalmist flashed into my mind: "The Lord is my shepherd; I shall not want." Though I could recall only that one verse at the moment, it was enough. I felt little fear as we lost momentum though we were coming perilously close to a crash landing. Knowing little about planes in trouble, I envisioned us tumbling tail over head, then crashing into terrain which would bring certain death, perhaps even a fiery one.

Then, it happened. Not the crash landing I had steeled myself for, but a touch down as smooth as that provided by a million dollar runway! We glided to a stop on the snow-covered Chena River, often referred to as just a slough. I was familiar with the Chena for it snakes its way through the city of Fairbanks. Still frozen that mid-March day, the Chena would have been a death trap of rotting ice in a matter of days.

The tower dispatched a small plane with sufficient gasoline to take us in and as the last vestige of daylight gave way to the night we touched down on the Fairbanks runway. God's miracle had pulled us through! Mable and I were in agreement that this was so. From her storehouse of Biblical promises, she declared: "God gave us His Word, 'I will never leave thee, nor forsake thee,' and He proved today He really meant it!" *

Then, Mable added, "Honey, God has more for us to do for Him--and I'm going to make every day count."

I backed her up: "Remember what Jesus said, 'The harvest truly is plenteous, but the labourers are few.'" **

Later, in the quiet of our home, we held a living room prayer meeting--just the two of us. Well, make that three. There's no escaping the fact that we felt the Presence of the Holy Spirit among us!

----

* Hebrews 13:5

** Matthew 9:37

Length of life possesses
little purpose until depth
assumes the role of
master of our days.

God Uses the Strangest Things!

(Mable)

I saw them coming! And I've never laid eyes on two little boys quite like them!

I just wanted to pick them up and squeeze them both. They came into my life and then were gone--all in a matter of minutes.

Edwin and I were spending a day or so in the pleasant little country of Costa Rica, a Central American republic snugly tucked between Panama and Nicaragua. Time permitted a sightseeing trip into the capital city of San José, a sprawling metropolis of magnificent cathedrals and spacious green parks. The minibus from our hotel dropped us off in the central business district, to pick us up later in the day.

The day had promised to be warm and my usually dignified tourist-husband had decided to shuck his coat, leaving it in our hotel room. We had no idea at the time how God was going to use that seemingly inconsequential decision.

While wandering about the downtown section of the placid city, Edwin and I stood in awe of the majestic cathedrals, we strolled about the plazas, we drifted in and out of intriguing little shops, making small purchases to accompany us home. After countless hours on our feet, I finally spied a lovely park and I plopped upon the nearest bench, planning to rest.

But there was no such thing. A constant procession of men plying their trade as bootblacks approached us, each man almost pleading to shine my husband's shoes. I felt compassion for these impoverished people as they attempted to eke out a miserable existence. Otherwise, I'm sure I would have given way to laughter at the absurdity of this novel "parade."

Then--out of nowhere--here they came! Two adorable little fellows, perhaps aged nine, each with his "business" strapped to his back. Seldom have I seen two happier children. Each wore an infectious grin as wide as his mouth would permit.

As my heart went out to them, I sensed that my dear spouse was equally moved. These two little merchants were capturing his heart.

The darling little lads knew not the first word of English--nor are we proficient in Spanish. But no problem. As both knelt in front of my husband, Edwin employed motions to indicate he was hiring one child to shine his right shoe, the other his left. To them the arrangement was simply hilarious and each labored to outdo his friendly competitor.

How I would love to witness to these precious children, I mused as I watched them complete their task. But--wouldn't you know it-- God was way ahead of me! Remember Edwin had doffed his coat before departing the hotel. This exposed his shirt pocket in which he had placed a colorful little booklet of poems entitled, "My Companion for Quiet Hours." On the cover of this devotional guide is the famous painting by Bernard Plockhorst. The painting is a masterpiece and is recognized world-wide as "The Good Shepherd."

Our Lord--shepherd's crook in His left hand--carries a thorn-infested lamb in the crook of His right arm. The mother sheep trots along by Jesus' side, keeping motherly eyes fixed upon her baby. I simply cannot observe this exquisite painting without experiencing a fresh love for my Saviour.

As our young friends put finishing touches on their work, each giving his shine rag that professional final "pop", they were still upon their knees. Suddenly, one of them looked up and discovered the little booklet protruding above my husband's pocket.

I thought the youngster was going to explode! He pointed to the painting of Jesus the Good Shepherd, then to heaven, then to his own heart. We had unknowingly witnessed to two small boys who only moments earlier had come into our lives. Now, we discovered, they knew Jesus as *their* Saviour, too!

I'm sure we appeared positively idiotic to strangers passing by! We gesticulated, we laughed, we hugged, we wiped away uncontrolled tears. This little drama was the highlight of our stay in Costa Rica.

Had not our bus driver begun honking rather persistently we'd have remained till dark! As our vehicle pulled away from the curbing with us aboard, Edwin and I leaned precariously far out the window until our young friends--waving their small arms off--were mere specks in the distance.

Back in our hotel room once more, I remarked, "What a strange thing God did today! He used something you and I would never have conceived of in order for us to proclaim our Christian faith!"

Edwin agreed. "And He did it without the use of one intelligible word!"

The incident just wouldn't leave me. "You know, honey," I declared later that evening, "I believe the Lord is telling us something! We should always identify ourselves as Christians through insignia on our clothing. It could be a cross, a cherub, an angel, or ---"

"Or the sign of the fish," Edwin affirmed, referring to an early-day means Christians used to identify themselves as followers.

Our experience with the small boys has proven to be just the first of a succession of opportunities to witness. At a cafeteria in Tennessee we identified ourselves as His followers through Christian insignia we were wearing. A God-fearing couple in the serving line right behind us became instant friends--not merely acquaintances--and have remained so across the years.

A Christian couple covering the country by motorcycle spied our crosses while we were in a National Park, resulting in a golden opportunity to share our faith.

And do you know, I'm convinced now that I should not even shop at a neighborhood grocery without wearing my Christian insignia. I just never know when God will use my silent witness and turn it into a fabulous opportunity to proclaim my faith in Him.

I always try to remember: *it is my declaration--not a decoration!*

How to Make the Bible "Fun"

(Edwin)

How many have ever considered Bible reading a "fun" experience? Often we think of it as a duty, sort of paying God back for His limitless mercies!

This should not be. Studying the Bible can be fun, educational, and a real blessing.

A while back, we discovered something we wish to share with you. It's a means of digging out spiritual gems from God's Word, a simple little game we play as we travel. Often there are just the two of us, although the game can be played just as easily with a group. No equipment is needed--except a Bible--and the game goes like this:

We begin by one of us taking the letter "A" and quoting a Bible verse which begins with that letter. We prefer the King James version simply because we "cut our spiritual teeth" on this version and through the years we have continued to study it more frequently than other translations.

Each of us takes a turn reciting a verse beginning with the letter "A" until we "exhaust our storehouse." We are amazed at how this simple little game sharpens the memory and brings to mind numerous verses that prove most meaningful. We prefer not to keep score, for one of the objects is to assist one another when we get "hung up" right in the middle of a verse.

We believe that you, too, will receive spiritual stimulation from this little game even if you travel alone. And of course if you do not travel it can be played at home or in a Sunday School class. Since our time is limited we find that the game fits our schedule best while we travel.

We will share with you some of our favorite verses--some of the better known perhaps. You may wish to expand your own "spiritual repertoire" by adding verses you will have to dig for.
Certain letters such as "B" with The Beatitudes to draw from seem almost limitless, while others (just wait till you come to "X") are harder to come by. Of course, it stretches the mind if you quote the reference as well. Mable and I most always include the following:

A.   "Ask, and it shall be given you; seek, and ye shall find; knock, and it shall be opened unto you" (Matthew 7:7).
"All things were made by him; and without him was not any thing made that was made: (John 1:3).
I must admit that we "cheat" a bit now and then by omitting the first word of a verse which begins with a preposition or conjunction. An example: "(For) all have sinned, and come short of the glory of God" (Romans 3:23).

B.   "Bless the Lord, O my soul: and all that is within me, bless his holy name" (Psalm 103:1).
"Behold, I stand at the door, and knock: if

any man hear my voice, and open the door, I will come in to him, and will sup with him, and he with me" (Revelation 3:20).

"Boast not thyself of tomorrow; for thou knowest not what a day may bring forth" (Proverbs 27:1).

C. "Come unto me, all ye that labour and are heavy laden, and I will give you rest" (Matthew 11:28).

"Casting all your care upon him; for he careth for you" (I Peter 5:7).

"Comfort ye, comfort ye my people, saith your God" (Isaiah 40:1).

D. "Draw nigh to God, and he will draw nigh to you" (James 4:8).

"Delight thyself also in the Lord; and he shall give thee the desires of thine heart" (Psalm 37:4).

(What about quoting *The Golden Rule?* "Do unto others as you would have them do unto you." We thought this was a good one until we checked it out: Matthew 7:12 and Luke 6:31. Look these up).

E. "Enter into his gates with thanksgiving, and into his courts with praise: be thankful unto him, and bless his name" (Psalm 100:4).

"Except the Lord build the house, they labour in vain that build it: except the Lord keep the city, the watchman waketh in vain" (Psalm 127:1).

(Under "E" we have stretched a point at times in order to quote a verse very special to us: "..., Eye hath not seen nor ear heard, neither have entered into the heart of man, the things which God hath prepared for them that love him" (I Corinthians 2:9).

F.   "For the wages of sin is death; but the gift of God is eternal life through Jesus Christ our Lord" (Romans 6:23).

"Finally, brethren, whatsoever things are true, whatsoever things are honest, whatsoever things are just, whatsoever things are pure, whatsoever things are lovely, whatsoever things are of good report; if there be any virtue, and if there be any praise, think on these things" (Philippians 4:8).

(Have you noticed a verse conspicuous by its absence? The Christian's favorite verse --so special we will come back to it later in the chapter).

G.   "Greater love hath no man than this, that a man lay down his life for his friends" (John 15:13).

"Go ye therefore, and teach all nations, baptizing them in the name of the Father, and of the Son, and of the Holy Ghost" (Matthew 28:19).

"Give to him that asketh thee, and from him that would borrow of thee turn not thou away" (Matthew 5:42).

H.   "Humble yourselves in the sight of the Lord, and he shall lift you up" (James 4:10).

"Herein is my Father glorified, that ye bear

much fruit; so shall ye be my disciples" (John 15:8).

"He that believeth on him is not condemned: but he that believeth not is condemned already, because he hath not believed in the name of the only begotten Son of God" (John 3:18).

I.   "I have fought a good fight, I have finished my course, I have kept the faith" (II Timothy 4:7).

"In every thing give thanks: for this is the will of God in Christ Jesus concerning you" (I Thessalonians 5:18).

"If ye abide in me, and my words abide in you, ye shall ask what ye will, and it shall be done unto you" (John 15:7).

J.   "Jesus saith unto him, I am the way, the truth, and the life: no man cometh unto the Father, but by me" (John 14:6).

"Judge not, that ye be not judged" (Matthew 7:1).

"Jesus answered and said unto him, Verily, verily, I say unto thee, Except a man be born again, he cannot see the kingdom of God" (John 3:3).

K.   "Keep thy heart with all diligence; for out of it are the issues of life" (Proverbs 4:23).

"Know ye not that ye are the temple of God, and that the Spirit of God dwelleth in you?" (I Corinthians 3:16).

L.   "Lay not up for yourselves treasures upon

earth, where moth and rust doth corrupt, and where thieves break through and steal" (Matthew 6:19).
"Let not your heart be troubled: ye believe in God, believe also in me" (John 14:1).
"Let this mind be in you, which was also in Christ Jesus" (Philippians 2:5).

M.   "Make a joyful noise unto the Lord, all ye lands" (Psalm 100:1).
"Marvel not that I said unto thee, Ye must be born again" (John 3:7).

N.   "Nicodemus saith unto him, How can a man be born when he is old? Can he enter the second time into his mother's womb, and be born?" (John 3:4).
"Now unto him that is able to keep you from falling, and to present you faultless before the presence of his glory with exceeding joy" (Jude 24).

O.   "O give thanks unto the Lord, for he is good: for his mercy endureth for ever" (Psalm 107:1 and 118:29).
"O sing unto the Lord a new song: sing unto the Lord, all the earth" (Psalm 96:1).
"Offer unto God thanksgiving; and pay thy vows unto the most High" (Psalm 50:14).

P.   "Pray without ceasing" (I Thessalonians 5:17).
"Praise ye the Lord: for it is good to sing praises unto our God" (Psalm 147:1).
"Peace I leave with you, my peace I give

unto you: not as the world giveth, give I unto you. Let not your heart be troubled, neither let it be afraid" (John 14:27).

Q.   "Quench not the spirit" (I Thessalonians 5:19).
"Quicken me, O Lord, for thy name's sake: for thy righteousness' sake bring my soul out of trouble" (Psalm 143:11).

R.   "Remember the sabbath day, to keep it holy" (Exodus 20:8).
"Rejoice in the Lord alway: and again I say, Rejoice" (Philippians 4:4).
"Restore unto me the joy of thy salvation; and uphold me with thy free spirit" (Psalm 51:12).

S.   "Study to shew thyself approved unto God, a workman that needeth not to be ashamed, rightly dividing the word of truth" (II Timothy 2:15).
"(But) seek ye first the kingdom of God, and his righteousness, and all these things shall be added unto you" (Matthew 6:33).
"Set your affection on things above, not on things on the earth" (Colossians 3:2).

T.   "This is my commandment, That ye love one another, as I have loved you" (John 15:12).
"That which is born of the flesh is flesh; and that which is born of the Spirit is spirit" (John 3:6).
"Teaching them to observe all things whatsoever I have commanded you: and,

lo, I am with you alway, even unto the end of the world. Amen" (Matthew 28:20).

U.   "Unto thee, O God, do we give thanks, unto thee do we give thanks" (Psalm 75:1).
"Use hospitality one to another without grudging" (I Peter 4:9).
"Unto him be glory in the church by Christ Jesus throughout all ages, world without end. Amen" (Ephesians 3:21).

V.   "Verily, verily, I say unto you, He that believeth on me hath everlasting life" (John 6:47).
"Verily, verily, I say unto you, He that believeth on me, the works that I do shall he do also; and greater works than these shall he do; because I go unto my Father" (John 14:12).

W.   "We love him, because he first loved us" (I John 4:19).
"Watch therefore: for ye know not what hour your Lord doth come" (Matthew 24:42).
"Whosoever shall confess that Jesus is the Son of God, God dwelleth in him, and he in God" (I John 4:15).

X.   It is up to you to find your own--we couldn't!

Y.   "Ye are my friends, if ye do whatsoever I command you" (John 15: 14).
"Yet a little while, and the world seeth me no more; but ye see me: because I live, ye shall live also" (John 14:19).

Z.   "Zion shall be redeemed with judgment, and
        her converts with righteousness" (Isaiah
        1:27).
        "(And) Zacchaeus stood, and said unto the
        Lord; Behold, Lord, the half of my goods I
        give to the poor; and if I have taken any
        thing from any man by false accusation, I
        restore him fourfold" (Luke 19:8).

Perhaps it has occurred to you that
numerous verses are taken from Chapter Three of
John's Gospel. One day, Mable declared, "That
chapter is fabulous! It's amazing how much Jesus
taught us in just the first half of Chapter Three." I
agreed. But more startling discoveries lay ahead.

In glancing over the Biblical index we
discovered there are 1,189 chapters from Genesis
through Revelation. Nothing unusual there, but
then we began noticing something most interesting.
In the Old Testament there are 929 chapters--just
71 short of being one thousand.

With her pencil moving faster and faster,
Mable began to add figures: "...929 plus 28 in
Matthew, 16 in Mark, and 24 in Luke. That totals
997! Then, listen to this: add chapters one, two,
and three!" My dear wife almost exploded.
"Honey, would you believe it! Chapter Three of
John's Gospel is *the one thousandth chapter in the
Bible!*" Both of us instinctively knew that Chapter
Three was special somehow. But here was a real
discovery!

The climactic verse in the chapter--and
perhaps the most beloved and most frequently
quoted verse in the entire Bible--is the 16th:

For God so loved the world, that He gave His only begotten Son, that whosoever believeth in him should not perish, but have everlasting life.

The word "whosoever" intrigues me! It's exciting! It's the same as writing MY name there and writing YOUR name there. No one is past being saved, no situation is hopeless. Eternal life is offered to everyone! But first we must BELIEVE--with no mental reservations. This word, so essential to salvation, winds its way all through the book of John, occurring more than ninety times.

If you have never made your commitment to Jesus, NOW is the time. Confess to Him that you accept Him as your Lord and Savior. Acknowledge Him as the only way to eternal life. The blood from His sinless veins will cover every sin you have committed. Remember--He died for *you* that you may never die. Salvation cannot be purchased; it cannot be earned through "good works." You simply accept it, and in doing so He gives you a peace that you may never have experienced.

No one making the decision has ever regretted it!